A Hand to Hold Along the Road

Lessons From The Backseat

Rena MCaffrey Henson

A Hand to Hold Along the Road: Lessons from the Backseat
First Edition
Copyright © 2012 by Rena McCaffrey Henson
ISBN# 978-1-4675-4063-6
Published by: Rena McCaffrey Henson
P.O. Box 145
House Springs, Missouri 63051
www.AHand2Hold.net

EDITOR AND CONCEPT DEVELOPMENT: Vincent M. Newfield
New Fields & Company
P. O. Box 622
Hillsboro, Missouri 63050
www.newfieldscreativeservices.com

COVER DESIGN: Marjorie McAllister
Web and Graphic Design
www.darksidecow.com

INTERIOR TEXT DESIGN: Lisa Simpson
Simpson Productions
www.simpsonproductions.net

ILLUSTRATION & ARTWORK: Mike Requa
requaink.net
1823 N. State Highway CC
Nixa, MO 65714

Printed in Canada.

Endorsements

Here's what some pretty cool people are saying:

Rena has found another "sweet spot" and created an exceptionally bold and refreshing, expression of faith and love. "If you could see where Jesus brought me from to where I am today, then you would know the reason why I love Him so!" These song lyrics sum up the depth of love Rena has for her Savior and for humanity. It's felt on each page and in each chapter. This book is not gender based and will relate to many ages, from teenagers to senior citizens.

Beverly Kuenzle
Former director of
Pregnancy Care Center of
Jefferson County, Missouri

Rena Henson's life-long battle with pain has brought her through so much that this book is a result. Within these pages are a combination of humor and inspiration with many "Rena-isms" interwoven. This is really a wonderful glimpse of a dear friend.

Paula Kersten
Program Director,
Teen Challenge of St. Louis,
Diane's House Women's Center

A tremendously anointed, easy-to-read book! I well remember the night of "Heaven's Gates and Hell's Flames," when Allen and Rena committed their lives to God and accepted Jesus Christ as their Savior. What a testimony of God's saving power! You won't be disappointed as you follow these lessons. May you find Christ as real and redemptive as Rena has.

Nora Ross
Rena's first devoted Christian
mentor and Staff Pastor,
New Hope Church,
Fenton, Missouri

A great read! Rena is an incredible example of God's saving grace! The fact that she is alive is a miracle. The story she tells will grip your heart. The lessons she shares will strengthen your soul. The Savior she loves will transform your life.

Vincent M. Newfield
Speaker, Freelance Writer, and Author,
New Fields Creative Services

Dedication and Prayer

I would like to dedicate this book to all my brokenhearted Sisters who still don't know that they have a *Hand to Hold*. I offer this prayer for you to the One who is ready to take hold of your hand when you are ready to let Him.

*Dear heavenly Father God, my **"ROCK"** and tender Lover of my soul...*

I pray for these women who are wounded and broken. Just as You have, and still are ministering these truths to me, I ask that you minister unto them.

*I pray that by the anointing of Your Holy Spirit, You will reveal to them the **Good News** in these pages. May You heal their broken hearts and cause them to see the things that still hold them captive. Set them free and help them remain free in You.*

As they learn of Your favor and grace, give them the power and desire to forgive and release those who have hurt them. Help them see that the day of vengeance is Yours—You will bring justice in Your time and Your way. As they turn these things over to Your care, I thank You for comforting them in their mourning and bringing them peace.

For those who grieve the loss of their childhood and innocence, I ask that You make provision for them, placing on their head a crown of beauty to replace the ashes of guilt and shame. As the spirit of despair and heaviness leaves, I thank You for covering them with Your oil of gladness and joy, placing a garment of praise upon them.

I praise You for making them "oaks of righteousness" in Your time—a planting of the Lord for the display of Your splendor (see Isaiah 61:1-3). I believe You will do this, not because of what they have or have not done themselves, but because of what You have already done on the cross!

In Your precious Son's name, Jesus, I pray. AMEN!

I encourage you to listen to "Beauty from Pain" by Superchick: http://www.youtube.com/watch?v=gqBMYoctFZM.

Acknowledgments

First and foremost, I want to give a huge shout out to Jesus for giving His all for me. Without His redeeming blood that bought me back from Satan, the very real enemy of our souls, I would not be alive today sharing His Good News!

I am also so very thankful for my husband, Allen. He is my example of Christ's love that never gives up. He is God's continued provision for me. He is my earthly rock! I love you!

To our daughters, Rachel and Sarah, thank you! I love you more than you will ever know. Thank you for helping me to become the woman I am today. You have both challenged and motivated me to be real and to love with God's kind of love.

I also want to thank my pastor, Ed Shirrell, Sunday school teachers and friends, who have all stood in the gap for me. They have held my hand, pointed me to our merciful Father, and been a priceless source of prayer and support.

To our photographer, Crystal Bandermann, our models, Sal and Natalie Hamdah, and to all of our riding buddies who blessed us with their time and kind cooperation for pictures that are on our website, AHand2Hold.net, thank you!

Lastly, I would like to thank our friend and editor, Vincent Newfield and his family. To say, "I trust you" is not something I take lightly. My dear friends, you have my trust! Thank you for being God's provision to me in laboring so graciously to make this dream a reality.

You are all "grace gifts" from God that I do not deserve. Thank you for your love, patience, and for not giving up on me. You share in the rewards of the fruit from this book. May your efforts in my life never be in vain!

~To God Be ALL the Glory for He is the true Rock Star!

Contents

Foreword

I have had the privilege of serving Rena and Allen since the night they found Jesus Christ at the Heaven's Gates & Hell's Flames drama. As their shepherd for the past two decades, they've attended a variety of classes with me, including one for new Christians, basic discipleship, spiritual gifts and a host of others. They are equipped followers of Christ.

Having a passion for motorcycles and a love for those coming to Jesus myself, I have found it easy to love on this couple. The first time I visited them after they received Christ, they gave me some "limited" insight into their past. When I asked Allen how he met Rena he said, "In sin, pastor." The transparency they displayed then is still refreshing today in their walk with the Lord.

I'll never forget the man that led me to Christ. He was a friend who wore leather, carried a leather Bible and rode a motorcycle. One day he asked me, "Ed, who is Jesus Christ to you? Either He's who He says He is, or He's a lunatic. If He is who He says He is, then you need to figure it out and make a decision about what you are going to do with Him." Because my biker friend had the guts to say what he said, I am who I am today—a child of God!

With genuine love, Rena and Allen have influenced, encouraged and discipled many for Christ as salt and light. They've walked the walk that matched their talk. In the midst of raising two lovely and talented daughters, they've overcome numerous obstacles and have produced lasting fruit. Truly they are trophies of God's grace, and I'm honored to be their friend and pastor.

Ed Shirrell
Senior Pastor, Faith Community Church,
House Springs, Missouri

Introduction

For many years, my life was one big mess. I was drinking, drugging, smoking and running. I knew nothing about peace or genuine love. I hopped from party to party and from man to man, but never found true enjoyment in life...until I met Jesus. He is awesome! He makes it clear that...

"The thief comes only in order to steal and kill and destroy. I came that they may have and enjoy life, and have it in abundance (to the full, till it overflows)."

—John 10:10 AMP

I know that there are many of you who have endured tremendous hurts and hardships. Satan has robbed you of the abundant life Jesus promised. I want to help.

The desire to help started one day years ago during a time of prayer when I was a new Christian. God showed me a vision that really freaked me out. I saw an uncountable sea of arms and hands reaching up from utter darkness for light. Quite shaken, I jumped to my feet and said, "I don't know what you want me to do with this God, but I think you've got the wrong chick!"

Twenty years later, that vision has never left my heart. I have cried many tears while interceding for those in darkness—including those in churches. I have not forgotten where I have come from. I too was once in darkness—great darkness. I was reaching for truth, light and something real to hold on to.

Before I found what I so desperately needed, I believed many misconceptions about God. I trusted the opinions and rants of others about a God they did *not* know. They were "unreliable messengers," and as Scripture says, "unreliable messengers cause trouble..." (Proverbs 13:17 GNT)

I also thought it was impossible to live for God. In my mind, to live for Him meant bondage—there were too many rules and regulations. I was not willing to give up what I thought was my freedom.

Lies like these are what the enemy of our soul wants us to believe. His only goal is to keep us from truth, and by doing so, keep us separated from our Creator and Father, God.

When I finally hit rock bottom twenty-one years ago, I was faced with the choice to give up or look up. I chose to look up and try the "God thing." When I did, I began to learn that everything I once thought true about God were nothing but lies. Freedom is not being able to do whatever you want to do. True freedom is having the power to do what's right.

At that point, I made a commitment to go to church faithfully every week. Instead of being in bed until noon with a hangover, I went to church—even when my family and friends made fun of me. I didn't go because I had to. I went because I wanted to. I had a hunger inside of me to learn what the Bible really said and why.

As time passed, I developed relationships with other Christians and learned to be transparent with them. I also began to understand what it meant to submit to the authority of the leaders God had placed in my life.

I'm so grateful that God stopped me dead in my tracks and helped me turn completely around. Through the power of His Holy Spirit, He has enabled me to make radical changes in my life, because radical change was what I needed. With great appreciation, I can now say I am sober and have lived smoke and drug free for over twenty years!

As you read through these lessons, know that God is with you. He wants to hold your hand if you will let Him. He says in His Word,

Introduction

"For I am the Lord your God who *takes hold of your right hand* and says to you, 'Do not fear; I will help you" (Isaiah 41:13 NIV).

God's love for you is real, His Word is relevant, and He wants to set you free to live abundantly! Open your hearts, dear friends, as you consider these lessons from my life, and see what God speaks to your heart.

TIPS FOR MAKING THE MOST OF THIS BOOK

This book is meant to be a tool to draw you closer to your heavenly Father, who loves you immensely. As you seek and enter into His presence, you will receive: salvation, healing, deliverance, and so much more. The Great I AM is everything you need Him to be.

The first lesson is a bit different from the rest, in that it includes a large part of my testimony up until the time I met Christ. Be warned: Some of the material is explicit and may not be suitable for younger readers. Please use discretion.

The six lessons that follow are real life stories tied to valuable principles the Lord has taught me. At the end of each lesson is a brief summary along with a few questions for your personal reflection or to discuss in a group. Take time to answer each question honestly and prayerfully. It's in these quiet times that God often brings transformation.

Because of the way God has used Christian music in my life, I have also included a playlist of songs that have been prayerfully chosen to help you absorb the truths presented. They can all be found on YouTube for free or purchased through iTunes at a minimal cost. They are intended to help you experience God's love and willingness to hold your hand through your deepest needs.

God bless you as you begin your journey!

~Rena

"You may never know that Jesus is all you need, until Jesus is all you have."

—Corrie Ten Boom[1]

Lesson 1

Rock My World...
Please!

"The Lord lives! Praise to my Rock! May God, the Rock of my salvation, be exalted!"

2 Samuel 22:47 NLT

We live about forty-five minutes southwest of St. Louis in a rural area with rolling hills as far as the eye can see. The neighbor's label on his home-spun honey jars reads "From the Foothills of the Ozarks". Without question, our surroundings are gorgeous.

My husband, Allen, and I love riding through these hills. As our girls, Rachel and Sarah, became old enough to stay home alone, we began taking quick little putts more often. "Let's take a ride around the block!" became our code for an hour-long excursion on the back roads.

Every time we ride I am overcome with God's goodness and a peaceful contentment that I rarely feel anywhere else. For years during these rides my attention has been focused on the expansive panoramic view. About ten years ago, that began to change. My view of the vast skyline was narrowed to a closer surveillance of the rocks along the road.

Actually, my attention to rocks grew into an insatiable obsession. The reason for this growing passion eluded me for years until one fateful day when we were blasting through the hills with the sound of our pipes drowning out the cares of the world. Again, my attention was drawn to the rocks. For the first time, I paused and asked, "What's going on Lord? Why am I so crazy about rocks?"

I had never received an answer from God as quickly as I did that day. Though it was silently impressed upon my heart, I heard it loud and clear, "Because *I am* your Rock."

Had I not been on the bike, I would have done the "Happy Dance" right there in the middle of the road! Limited in my range of motion, I still managed to do a back seat version without causing Allen to drop the bike. It was hard to contain all that was going on inside of me at that moment.

Think about it! The Lord God Almighty, Creator of heaven and earth personally whispered to me that He was my ROCK!

How could anyone sit still and not be moved by the "Rock of Ages" speaking to them?

You see, for most of my life, my existence was anything but stable. Pandemonium and chaos would be a better description. Not only was I living out of control, I also came to a point when I denied God's existence and later purposed to live for Satan.

God truly has brought some rock-solid stability to my life. With great gratitude, I began to reflect on the things from which He has rescued me. The following is a brief summary of my life before Jesus. Warning: Some of the following testimony is explicit and may not be suitable for younger readers. Please use discretion.

MY SHAKY FAMILY FOUNDATION

My brother and I recently spent two weeks attempting to piece together our sparse childhood memories. I am thankful to God that I don't have a complete memory of my past. I believe it is His mercy. As memories do surface, I continue to depend on my mom, who is now a Christian, to verify them.

One of the things she told me about my childhood was that the first time I ran away from home I was on my tricycle. I don't remember that, but I do remember running away when I was about five. I walked down our gravel road with a brown grocery sack full of clothes. The bag ripped with every step I took, leaving a trail of clothes in the dust behind me. Running would become my way of life.

When my brother was seven and I turned nine, our parents told us of their plans to separate. We both sobbed as our world was ripped apart. Ours may not have been the best family but it was ours and the only thing we knew. We pleaded with them to not let this happen. We made our dad promise to come back. That was our first lesson that promises meant nothing; they were made to be broken.

At that time, things began to really get crazy. My parents' separation was the bomb that blew the lid off any resemblance of sanity and structure. Without my father, the God-appointed protector of our family, we were left unguarded and vulnerable. This proved to be even more impacting in the absence of a moral and godly foundation at home.

My dad abandoned the religion he had been raised in when he was eighteen. He then dabbled in many occult practices, including witchcraft, alchemy and pyramid power. My mother had minimal upbringing in the church. At one point her mom attended a church in the backwoods where snake handling was common.

My mom's father came from a very superstitious family, in which his mother read tea leaves. He was diagnosed in the 70s as a paranoid schizophrenic suffering from manic depression. After shooting his sister's dog, while she was holding it, he was sentenced to a state mental institution.

All in all, my mother received very little affection from her parents and had no solid foundation of her own. As a result, it was easy for her to follow my dad into a life of selfish, godless living. The seeds of her family heritage eventually sprang up, leading her to live by horoscopes, psychics and tarot card readings for quite some time.

Because our family was without a firm foundation my brother and I were left vulnerable to everything against the name of the Most High God. Jesus described the results of this condition in the Gospel of Luke:

> **"The one who hears my words and does not put them into practice is like a man who built a house on the ground without a foundation. The moment the torrent struck that house, it collapsed and its destruction was complete."**
>
> **—Luke 6:49 NIV**

Complete was the destruction of our family's home causing my brother and I to eventually gravitate to the same occult practices, only to take them to a higher level. Void of anything to really hold on to, I tried almost everything you can imagine at least once. The problems I would encounter as a result over the next eighteen years were beyond anything I could have imagined. It is only God's grace that kept me alive.

SUCKED INTO A WHIRLWIND OF SIN

Once my mom and dad officially parted ways, my brother and I were tossed back and forth between them. During the week we were with Mom, and every other weekend we were with Dad. When we were around her, she verbally assassinated him. When we were with him, he did the same to her. Our lives were one big rollercoaster ride of emotions as we cried and begged our mom to not make us go to our dad. After two weeks of hearing what a bad person he was, why would she make us go? The same happened after we spent our time with dad, only we didn't want to go back to our mom because of what he had said about her.

Meanwhile, my mom had to go to work so we'd have money to live. This meant we were often left to fend for ourselves. When she did manage to have sitters for us, they were young teenagers from our neighborhood. Just kids themselves, they did the best they could. But there was plenty of partying that went on. My sweet little brother hid in his room trying to escape, while I followed in their footsteps wholeheartedly.

I began hitchhiking with one of our sitters at the age of nine. Since she and the others smoked and drank beer, I smoked and drank beer—regularly. As strange as it may seem, my mom began keeping gallon jugs of hard liquor for our babysitters to have at their disposal. I helped myself to this as well.

I had just finished third grade when all these things started happening. It was also at this time that I began experimenting sexually. I honestly can't tell you if anything happened before that because I don't have many memories before this. What I can say is that I knew nothing of boundaries and neither did anyone else—including the "adults."

My father started watching lewd and pornographic movies with me, as well as movies filled with occult practices during our weekend visits and summer vacations. He treated me like an adult. While in public, he pretended I was his girlfriend and my little brother was our son. He would kiss me on the mouth and on my ears while making growling sounds. To this day I can't stand to have my ears kissed or messed with like he did.

At night, he demanded that I wear nightgowns, and if I didn't he would whip me. He expected me to listen to his problems as he cried on my shoulder in the middle of the night. I was incapable of carrying his emotional burdens. Thankfully, I don't remember any sexual contact from him physically like many of you may have had to endure. Nevertheless, the mental and emotional abuse left a lasting effect.

The lack of boundaries mixed with a seemingly endless supply of drugs, alcohol and pornography was a recipe for more progressive behavior with others in private. The crazy spin the bottle games with neighborhood kids got wilder each time I played. This eventually led to me being attacked outside on the dirt hills near my house.

In the place where I once played carefree, riding bikes and playing King of the Hill, a group of boys and girls tore my clothes off and assaulted me. Soon afterward two of the boys tried to do the same thing again while we were playing in the woods. I fought as hard as I could during both incidences. My attackers eventually gave up leaving me to drown in my tears and shame as I tried to put my clothes back on. This was only the beginning of the countless violent attacks I would experience before I was married.

DEEPER AND DEEPER I SANK

By the age of ten, I was sneaking out and blacking out from alcohol. The summer between fifth and sixth grade I started smoking pot. Somewhere around this time is when "follow the party" began to be my motto, and there was no shortage of those in sight.

The progression into harder drugs easily increased after my best friend and I began raiding medicine cabinets in sixth grade. We would take prescription and over-the-counter medications randomly. Not knowing what they were, we swallowed them "Russian Roulette" style.

By seventh grade, I added several more drugs to my menu, including joints laced with angel dust (PCP), hash and acid (LSD). The next summer was spent driving around in a van fueled with gas siphoned from any car that was an easy target. We added to this madness the "choking game." We took turns huffing (breathing in quickly) the fumes of the stolen gas and then being squeezed around the chest. Deprived of oxygen, we would get a crazy rush and then pass out briefly.

Amidst all this, my sexual escapades continued. Although my innocence had already been long lost, I technically gave away my virginity at age twelve. While blacked out at a party, I came to during the act. Half-conscious I asked, "You love me, don't you?" He laughed at me and continued his assault. Sex with older guys and married men became typical after that. This may come as a surprise to some, but there was an endless line of married men and those even professing to be Christians. I was desperately searching for someone to love me, but the only thing I succeeded at becoming was the neighborhood slut.

At age thirteen, I started running away and getting kicked out of my house regularly. I hitchhiked everywhere and began living on the streets, roaming the town like a crazy homeless person. I went from one party to the next following any prospect of love. Once when I was extremely intoxicated I was pimped out by a guy who I thought liked me. We met when he picked me up hitchhiking. All I wanted was for him to love me, but true love was always out of reach.

When I got away from him, I ended up with an older man for a couple of weeks. Once he realized I was only thirteen, he ditched me at some apartments about five miles from my mom's house. This wild party place was known as "The Spot." The people who lived there found me asleep in the stairwell and took me in like a stray cat. The living conditions were basically "commune style" with plenty of sex, drugs and rock-n-roll to go around. It was here I experienced mescaline for the first time, which is a hallucinogenic drug in powder form that is snorted.

Again, I had no godly example or boundaries. In fact, the woman I lived with was a bartender at a dance bar named Queen of Hearts. At the age of thirteen, I was helping her stock the bar during her day shift, and while the girls put on their "fashion shows," I was given shots of liquor.

After partying for several months with this group, I ended up in the hospital with a severe kidney infection. Not knowing who to release me to after I told them about things going on at home, they kept me for a week until the Division of Family Services forced me to live with my dad. I was out of the frying pan and into the fire.

NO EARTHLY CURE

I was now fourteen, and as you can probably imagine, I was an emotional basket case. Not knowing how to handle me, my father took me to the highest acclaimed child psychiatrist in the St. Louis area. During each high-priced session, she would talk with me over a game of chess, trying to understand what was going on inside. As soon as she found out that I had held a switchblade to my brother's throat and threatened to slice him if he told on me, she recommended that I be placed in a lock-up for mental evaluation.

For two months I was confined to St. Vincent's de Paul Hospital. During that time I was prescribed antidepressants and an increased dosage of valium to calm me down. On many occasions I was escorted to the white-padded cell called the "quiet room" and placed in restraints. When I attempted to escape, it took six security guards to catch me and hold me down. As they tried to buckle the restraints, I broke one of the guard's glasses and busted his nose.

Ironically, during my stay I began using a hypodermic needle to take drugs. A patient who claimed to be a Satan worshipper had returned with a rig after receiving a weekend pass. He had cleverly removed the guts from an 8-track cassette and replaced it with a syringe and tie-off strap. We would save the medication they gave us, crush it, mix it with water and mainline it with the contents of the 8-track we passed back and forth.

But when a very large attendant found me in my bathroom with my arm tied off and the rig (needle) about to hit its target, my days at St. Vincent's were over. As they drug me down the hall, I managed to get one arm loose, and with a closed fist I backhanded the nurse square in the face with everything I had in me. Needless to say, I was kicked out of the program.

Released again into my dad's custody, I continued my rebellious ways. One day he lost complete control of his temper and tore into me giving me my first bloody nose. Not that I didn't deserve to be punished, but I was barely recognizable when my friend and her mom intervened. Again, I planned to run away.

Two weeks later, I hitchhiked to Los Angeles, California. I did whatever I needed to do to survive, including paying my way across the country with sex. But because of some unexpected craziness and a rare moment of fear, I immediately turned around and hitchhiked back to St. Louis. I spent a couple of weeks with a friend that lived near my dad, and then again began to hop around from party to party. Eventually I ended up living with some of the same people from "The Spot" in a different apartment and then moved with them again into a bigger house. This way more people could live with us and share in the 24/7 party.

Around that time I became totally disgusted with myself. In my mind, I concluded that if God did exist, He was doing a lousy job with my life. I was a ball of uncontrollable urges and emotions. Since nobody wanted me, I decided to sell my soul to the devil.

It was nighttime and I was hungry, we always had drugs but rarely had food. So I decided to go to my mom's house to get something to eat. It was made known that I was only to stay the night. While alone in my old room later that evening, I said out loud, "Satan, if you want me you can have me, because no one else wants me." I then vowed that I didn't need anyone to take care of me ever again, especially a man.

No sooner had the words left my mouth, I sensed the terrorizing presence of an evil spirit come upon me and assaulted me. It is hard to put into words what took place and the great fear that gripped my soul. Crying hysterically, I managed to get away and run to my mom's room. There I sat on the floor, paralyzed by fear until sunrise. I would experience this frightful encounter two or three times more. Only the grace of God could deliver me from the enemy's clutches.

REJECTED AND UNWANTED

I continued to live my life fast and hard. I got busted selling acid at fifteen and spent the night in jail. Again, I waited for the authorities to figure out what to do with me. They sent me for my second stay at a juvenile detention center. Eventually, I was released to my mom.

I went back to school, but the only reason I went was to sell enough pot to supply my own habit. I became severely depressed and attempted suicide twice. Unconscious from a drug overdose during the second attempt, I was carried away in an ambulance to have my stomach pumped. I was then sent to the lockup ward of another hospital.

At this point my mom could take no more. Afraid she would come home to find me dead, she gave up custody to the state. I stayed in the hospital lockup for about a month. I was then placed in an orphanage in Farmington, Missouri for almost two months. Just like everywhere else I had been, I could not be controlled. When I was busted with pot, I was quickly placed into a foster home where I lived for five months.

The only good thing that came out of my foster stay was that I met Allen while there. We saw each other at a tavern nearby. He was drinkin' and druggin' just like me. There were no fireworks and it was not love at first sight. But he was one of the only people I knew who showed me any genuine care. Sadly, I was too emotionally numb to recognize and appreciate it.

My intense hatred for myself and life could not be quenched, and once again history repeated itself. With another attempt at suicide, I was carried away from the foster home in an ambulance once more. My slashed wrist was stitched up and I was temporarily placed back at St. Vincent's de Paul. Knowing I had wounded two of their staff members the last time I was there, they escorted me out the door as soon as they could.

I returned to the foster home where my future was uncertain. Not wanting to be placed somewhere out of my control, I ran away again. I continued to drink and party, adding crystal meth, cocaine and several different kinds of speed to the ever growing list of drugs I used.

I reconnected again with the woman I had lived with off and on beginning when I was thirteen. She had found another house and was living on Lake Loraine near Hillsboro, Missouri. The partying continued, and I began using Quaaludes. But this living arrangement only lasted a few months. My constant drunkenness and out of control behavior was even too much for the "free living" commune crowd.

When I got kicked out, I moved across the lake and lived with a man named Duke. He had become our main source for all things illegal, including the prescription pain pills called Dilaudids. We referred to them as Ds and knew them to be a synthetic form of heroin, which we mainlined. I started driving the getaway car with a couple of guys doing home burglaries. Duke fenced the stolen goods and supplied all the Ds, pot and booze we wanted. At the same time, he was grooming me to begin working at a "massage parlor" where his girlfriend and several others that I knew worked.

After learning some "tricks of the trade" and going out on some practice runs, I hitchhiked to the massage parlor where I would become a fulltime prostitute. Ironically, when I reached the exit, I had a moment of mental clarity. Although I was stoned out of my gourd, I knew I needed to get away from there as fast as I could.

I ran across the highway and started hitchhiking in the opposite direction of the parlor. I never went back to stay with Duke. Instead, I went straight to a girlfriend's house not too far away and hid out there until I was seventeen. At that age, I was released from the state's custody and finally on my own. It's only by God's grace I survived all I went through. He saw value in my life even when I couldn't.

Hooking Up with Allen

I lived many more years running from myself and drowning in massive amounts of drugs and alcohol. At one point I had become an alcorexia alcoholic or as I called it an alcorexic. I ate very little if anything while drinking like a fish. Thankfully, one night a guy I was seeing and a friend of his who had also been through anorexia, force fed me a steak. I continued to drink, but their efforts helped me to start eating again.

Then at age nineteen, I moved in with Allen who is now my husband. We had hung out together off and on since we met. After a brief fling when I was sixteen, we ended up friends looking to have a good time in between other relationships. All that changed as we grew closer when I was eighteen and then began to live together.

Still yet, life was one big party. We spent all our free time in bars or at a bash of some sort which was often at our house. I tried hard, yet rarely succeeded, at maintaining a moderate level of sedation to keep the anger that simmered inside of me from boiling over. But it was unstoppable.

Volatile is not even close to describing our relationship. Neither of us knew anything about dealing with conflict. His periodic attempts to resolve issues were met with my extremely defensive responses. I felt attacked or that he was intruding in my "bidness," and I would immediately go on autopilot-attack mode. I was prepared to defend myself at any cost and had no desire to back down.

Thankfully, Allen never physically abused me. In fact, the opposite is true. When my rage boiled over, he would often sit on me—not only to protect himself, but also to protect me from myself. One time I sent him to the hospital with a gash in his leg that needed stitches, and another time I tried to take his head off with a loaf of frozen bread. I hurled it like a rocket right at him. Fortunately, I missed him and busted out our kitchen window instead.

Though we loved one another in our limited understanding of what love was, we just didn't know how to make it work. In an attempt to fix things between us, we got married two years after we moved in together. However, this did not fix what was broken. The peace and real love we both longed for eluded us. We couldn't give to each other what we didn't have.

Hope Appears on the Horizon!

Mentally exhausted, I was at the end of my rope and grasping for hope. In addition to the constant fighting, uncontrollable rage and addictions, I had also been seeing shadows of beings around me. This actually started in seventh grade when I began taking acid. On more than one occasion when I was hitchhiking, I had seen a huge, ape-like creature following me on the opposite side of the road. All I knew to do in those moments of terror was to sing the only line of a song I had learned as a child at my cousin's church—"Yes, Jesus Loves Me."

Desperate, I finally told a friend that was living with us at the time about some of these strange spiritual experiences I was having. I cried as she shared with me a personal experience she had had with Jesus. No one had ever told me anything so encouraging or that rang truer within my soul. A seed of hope had been planted. I was twenty-two.

A year later, while pregnant with our oldest daughter I went to church for the first time since I was in the orphanage. God knew exactly what I needed to hear when He used my friend. I went to church because of her, even though she wasn't a perfect Christian example and wasn't in church every time the doors were open.

When it was time for prayer, I practically ran to the altar and surrendered all the heavy guilt and shame I had carried for so long. Right then and there, I received God's free gift of grace—His forgiveness and salvation through Jesus' death and resurrection. Driving home, I felt very different. For the first time since I could remember, I felt lighthearted and full of joy. Peace filled my soul and I didn't feel dirty. I felt shiny, new and clean through and through.

Although I didn't see it at the time things truly changed that day, but mainly on the inside where others could not see. I began to think of Jesus more often. I also tried to read my Bible and go to church... even though it was only once or twice a year. Unfortunately, I was still hanging out in bars where fights had a way of finding me. Thankfully, I had quit looking for them.

Without discipleship over the next four years, I picked up everything I had laid on the altar when I accepted Christ. On most days I drank the better part of a twelve pack before Allen got home from work. This served to kick things off as we partied well into the night. During this phase of my life, I added my own prescription pain pills to the list of drugs I was taking, of which I had an unlimited supply. Life was a tiny bit better, but it was still far from what it should be.

AND A LITTLE CHILD SHALL LEAD THEM

I guess by now you have figured out that I probably wasn't the best mother to my sweet little girls, and you are right. But I was the best mother I knew how to be. We weren't rich but we also weren't poor. We made sure all of their physical needs were met and there was always plenty of food on the table. Although things were clean, they were by no means sanitary. How we didn't die from food poisoning is truly a miracle of God.

Nothing in my life motivated me to do better than being a parent. I desperately wanted to be a good mommy, one of the only things I allowed myself to have hope in. This drove me to use more self-control than ever before. During both pregnancies, I managed to almost quit smoking. I still drank but nowhere near what I had before my pregnancies. I tried to follow my doctor's orders of one drink a day, but I almost always pushed the limit to one extra.

The real problems started when the girls became old enough to start saying no. Their normal childhood defiance enraged me. As you might have guessed, they had the most energy and showed their greatest rebellion when I was plastered to the couch because of a hangover. The fights I had with their dad caused me to be even more impatient with them. As a result, I began whipping them out of anger.

Oh yes, I was a screamer. I later learned that screaming is hereditary. What I received from my parents I passed on with ease to the next generation. Each day I grew more and more frustrated. Anger and bitterness were building inside of me like a pressure cooker. At that point I started being tormented with thoughts of killing my kids, my husband, and then myself.

On one occasion, these thoughts just about overtook me. I was peeling potatoes in the kitchen and the girls were in the other room fighting. The louder they got, the louder the thoughts became. Suddenly, my eyes became fixed on the glimmering knife in my hand. Then just as quickly, I heard a completely different voice in my head say, "That is Satan!" Immediately, the rage melted and I began to cry. I forced the knife from my hand and onto the cutting board.

I ran into the other room, grabbed my girls and hugged them tightly. I knew in that moment I had to get us to church no matter what. I also knew the church we had to go to. It wasn't the one I had gone to a handful of times before. It was the one that I drove by regularly—the one with the ever-changing marquee I always loved to read. The truth in those messages ministered to my heart again and again, leading me to the place God wanted our family.

I purposed with everything in me to be at that church the following Sunday. The gift of my children became the catalyst to lead me back to God for good.

POINTED IN THE RIGHT DIRECTION

Unfortunately we didn't make it to church as planned. Following through on things I committed to rarely happened. But God didn't give up on me. He knew what I needed and sent me the perfect messenger that Sunday afternoon to point me in the right direction.

A very good friend of ours came over and brought his former girlfriend who we used to party with. She and I had many things in common from our past. She handed me a folded piece of paper and said, "I feel I'm supposed to give you this."

As I opened it, I saw that it was a bulletin from the morning service of the church I knew we were supposed to go to. I got chills. I knew God was directing me. I'm so thankful He sent her to help me gain the courage I needed to keep heading in the direction my heart knew I needed to go. With God's help, my oldest daughter, Rachel and I went to church the following Sunday.

I cried through the whole service. At the end, when the invitation was given to come and pray at the altar, I remained in my seat crying. I had been there and done that. To my spiritually untrained eyes, nothing seemed to have really changed. I believed that if I had gone up for prayer and nothing would have changed, I would have been devastated. So much so, that I was terrified of what I would do to my husband, my girls or myself.

I left the church that day promising God I would quit smoking and drinking. I desperately wanted to get a hold of myself and live right, but I was trying to do it in my own strength.

A TEMPORARY DETOUR

Will power alone will only take a person so far as I quickly learned. I did really well for several days until we went out the following Friday night with Allen's cousin and his girlfriend.

The restaurant and bar were both packed—standing room only. When we managed to squeeze up to the bar, Allen went to the restroom leaving Jimmy to ask me what I wanted to drink.

With my gaze fixed on a passing tray of margaritas, I replied, "I'll have an iced tea." Jimmy laughed at me.

By this time my man returned. Since we still had not been waited on, he too asked me, "What do you want to drink?"

My mouth was watering for a margarita, but I gave him the same answer, "I'll have an iced tea." Allen laughed at me as well.

As you may have guessed, I didn't drink one iced tea that night. Instead, as we celebrated the announcement of an upcoming wedding, we drank three pitchers of margaritas. Well, three of us did anyway. I finished Allen's toast drink and he switched to beer.

Later that night we ended up at a keg party. Still drinking and smoking, I stumbled around telling everyone how I was taking my kids to church. After consuming copious amounts of alcohol and smoking three packs of cigarettes, I ended up in the emergency room with severe abdominal pain. I was tested and monitored from 1:30 a.m. to 6 a.m. The final diagnosis given: bladder spasms.

So much for my will power.

TOTAL SURRENDER…A NEW BEGINNING!

We made it home early in the morning Saturday. Still sick and hung over Sunday, the girls and I missed church again. However, I remembered that the church was putting on a special drama that week called, "Heaven's Gates and Hell's Flames." Amazingly, I got up enough courage to ask Allen to go with me and even more amazingly, he agreed.

I'll never forget that night. The atmosphere of the church was saturated with God's tangible presence. Each scene of heaven and hell was vividly real. When it came time for the altar call, Allen got up out of his seat without any hesitation. When I managed to catch up to him, I took his hand and we hit the altar together.

That night in 1991, my husband was born again. Just like I had done four years earlier, Allen repented of his sins and invited Jesus into his life. It would take another six months before he fully surrendered to God, but there was a marked change in his character from then on.

For me, that night brought about a total surrender to God. I knew what I had been doing wasn't working. I was ready to do things God's way and yield to His Lordship. If the Bible said it, I was gonna believe it, and to the best of my ability I was gonna live it. When I gave up control of my life, Jesus came in and *rocked my world!*

"...The Lord is my rock, my fortress and my deliverer; my God is my rock, in whom I take refuge..."

—2 Samuel 22:2-3 NIV

Without question, "He lifted me out of the slimy pit, out of the mud and mire; He set my feet on a rock and gave me a firm place to stand" (Psalm 40:2 NIV).

Things on the outside of my life finally began to change. That night, God totally delivered me from drugs, cigarettes and alcohol. I never drank, smoked or did nonprescription drugs ever again! God knew I didn't know how to live life without these things, so He supernaturally took the desire away.

Our Pastor's teaching on real life issues that were based on the foundation of scripture began to take root in my heart. I also got involved in a few different Christian twelve-step programs over the years, each helping me at just the right time. Another powerful connection was made when God led me to Joyce Meyer's TV and radio program. A victim of sexual abuse herself, I could fully relate to her. Some of the titles of her life changing messages have changed over the years from when I first was ministered to by them. However, I highly recommend these updated versions: *Dying to Live, Freedom from Co-Dependency, Grace, Grace and More Grace, The Truth about Obedience, Beauty for Ashes*, and *One Life* formerly titled *Trophies of Grace-Joyce's personal testimony.*

There are more life changing materials for you to check out in the section titled Resources of this book. I have found all of these materials to be full of God's truth. I know you have heard that, "the truth will set you free," but that is only a half truth. According to God's Word, the truth will only set us free as we hold on to Jesus' teachings and begin to apply them to our lives (John 8:31,32 NIV).

As I began to apply these truths in God's word and through the power of the Holy Spirit, along with the prayers and help of many, I have been growing spiritually ever since I allowed God access into all areas of my life. Miraculously, my life has never been the same because the Great I Am is MY ROCK!

Lesson Summary

Something to Hold On To

Before I surrendered to Jesus, my life was one huge mess. I experimented with virtually every drug imaginable and had been with more men than I can remember. I was drunk more days than I was sober, experienced more car accidents and fights than I can count, and even let guys beat me up over and over. The physical scars I have, and they are many, are external wounds of a life without a solid foundation built on Jesus Christ and yet, the deeper scars were left within my soul. My actions and attitudes before Christ were not the problem; they were the symptoms of the internal damage that had been done. There was a hole in my heart crying out to be filled. Only the love and grace of its Creator would ever be enough to fill it.

Through all the professional counseling sessions and the plethora of medications I received, nothing calmed the storm that raged inside of me. Instead of getting better, I moved farther into depravity without any conscience or remorse. Only when the Great I Am gave me a solid footing and a hand to hold did I find peace.

Maybe you are like I once was, tired and hanging at the end of your rope about to let go. Dear friend it's time to let go of the rope of the past and grab the hope found in Christ Jesus. Free-fall into His constant, unchanging, dependable and everlasting arms of love. Don't put it off. Surrender to Him today!

Rena's playlist:

- "Everything" ~ by Lifehouse – skit- http://www.youtube.com

- "Lead Me to the Rock" ~ by Word of God Speak

- "You Led Me" ~ by Barlow Girl

- "Jesus, Lover of My Soul" ~ by Darlene Zschech

Questions for personal or group reflection:

- What kind of moral and spiritual foundation did you have while growing up? What was the climate of your home (parental/sibling relationships)? How is it affecting you today?

- Pause and reflect over your life. Can you see the hand of God? Are there things He protected you from or delivered you out of? What are they? How does it make you feel?

- Have you repented of your sins and invited Jesus into your life? Have you asked Him to be your Savior but not made Him Lord? If so, what's hindering you from total surrender?

- Have you made vows or taken oaths that need to be recanted/renounced? If so, write them down, ask for God's forgiveness, and renounce them in the name of Jesus. Ask your pastor, a godly elder, or someone in spiritual authority to pray blessings over you.

- What is your greatest "take away" from this lesson— what came alive and jumped off the pages that you want to remember?

---

[1]_Quotes about Jesus Christ_ (http://dailychristianquote.com/dcqjesus2.html, accessed 6/21/12).

"God will help you be all you can be, but He will never let you be successful at becoming someone else."

—Joyce Meyer[1]

Lesson 2

Sweet Spots:
Where's Yours?

For we are God's masterpiece. He has created us anew in Christ Jesus, so we can do the good things he planned for us long ago.

Ephesians 2:10 NLT

I love road trips. Just put me on a Harley with my hubby and I am in heaven! On this trip, which you will hear a lot about throughout the book, Allen and I were headed to Rocky Mountain National Park, Colorado. The mission: get some much needed R&R.

Allen's brother had graciously loaned us his truck. Our plans were to trailer the bike from just outside of St. Louis to North Platte, Nebraska where we would meet up with our good friend Keith. While there, we planned to drop the truck and trailer and ride to the mountains to play for a few days.

With the bike and gear in place and some great tunes blasting, we were ready to conquer the many miles ahead. Thinking Allen would be occupied with driving, I grabbed my laptop with the hope of knocking out some pages for this book. I got myself comfy, fluffing my pillows and arranging my snacks within reach. I had barely cracked open my computer when Allen asked, "What are you doing?"

Instantly, I felt a familiar twinge in my gut—an uneasiness I had felt so many times before when asked to share anything creative. I had recently gained major ground in this area. For the first time I was beginning to have confidence while sharing creative ideas with others, including my husband. By God's grace, I fought off the temptation to say something I would have regretted and casually explained, "I am going to work on the book I told you about."

I then held my breath in hopes that would be the end of it. But instead of dropping it, Allen continued with more questions—a move I would have considered an interrogation in times past.

This time, however, was different. I made a choice to believe the best and kick all the negative thoughts to the curb. My fears were quieted as he not only listened intently, but also encouraged me in a supportive way. His growing, sincere interest caused me to open up more and more—my voice becoming stronger with each idea we exchanged.

With confidence, I proceeded to read to him what I had written so far, listing the titles of each lesson until I came to this one. At that time, the working title was "Where's Your Sweet Spot?" with its main focus on where we spend time with God in prayer.

Much to my surprise, Allen stopped me and asked, "Do you know where the *sweet spot* is on a motorcycle?"

He now had my attention. My ears perked up like our dog's ears do when we ask if she wants a chewy treat. He continued, "It's not just motorcycles that have sweet spots. Every vehicle has one."

At that point, the hair on the back of my neck and arms stood up. Until that moment, I had not heard of sweet spots in a mechanical context. I was now fully engaged. My loving man and I then shared one of those rare moments you dream about having. The connection was unreal. Our pistons were firing rapidly, and we were hitting on all cylinders.

WHAT DID I LEARN ABOUT *SWEET SPOTS* THAT DAY?

➢ Basically, a "sweet spot" occurs when each component of a larger unit is first balanced individually and then balanced with all the other parts as a whole. When they come together at just the right speed and at just the right time they become synchronized as one unit, functioning with amazing smoothness.

> ➢ Sweet spots can vary from vehicle to vehicle. The same make and model may have a certain amount of variances in its different parts even if they are minute.

> ➢ Sweet spots will be different, depending on what the vehicle is made for—specifically the load it is built to carry.

THE FIRST STEP TO FINDING MY SWEET SPOT

At the age of twenty-six and many years before this road trip, I had hit rock bottom. I was ready for a change in my life. Doing things "the same old, same old" way wasn't going to cut it. I had been drunk, drugging and extremely dysfunctional for the majority of my life. I did what I wanted, when I wanted, and it clearly wasn't working. I was more than ready to do things God's way.

But what did "God's way" look like? I didn't know, and I was even more clueless how to do it. What I *did* know was that I was desperate for change and freedom, and it was time to allow Jesus to be *Lord* of my life, not just my Savior. I not only needed Him to forgive me of my sins, but also to show me how to live.

In His tender mercy, God directed me to a place where I could gain this understanding—a good Christian church. As I said in the first lesson, I knew that I knew that was what my daughters and I needed. God got my undivided attention when an old friend I used to party with dropped by our house the Sunday I had planned to go to church, but didn't. She had surrendered her life to God and was going to church—the same church I felt God was leading me to. When she handed me the church bulletin from that morning's service, a chill ran through me. God was speaking. The following Sunday we were there.

At that point, I had no thought of trying to make my husband go with us. Somehow I knew that if I focused on him in any way I would not follow through. So I focused my attention on our girls and myself. I continued doing the first thing I knew God wanted me to do—go to the church He led us to. The second thing I knew I was supposed to do was keep my butt there! No church hopping. Beyond that, I wasn't sure what God's plan was for me or the capacity in which He created me to function. But I would soon begin to learn.

I was sober for the first time in a long while. Suddenly, the woman I had become mattered to me. What bothered me even more was the person I was not. For the first time since I was a girl, I wanted to be someone who did things the right way. I wanted to be a good example for our daughters to follow. I wanted people to be proud of me and believe in me. I was alive and starting to grow in the right direction. But challenges awaited.

DEALING WITH THE DISEASE OF PEOPLE PLEASING

Going to church each week was feeding my spirit in ways I had never experienced. I was learning things I had never heard. For instance, I didn't know what a "principle" was. I thought it was the dude at school with a paddle at the end of his arm that often found its way to my rear. I also learned what integrity was, and when I did, I realized that I didn't have any.

Yes, the truth can be painful at times, but with God's grace it eventually brings healing.

Healing and restoration was and still is our pastor's motivation. His heart to help new Christians discover their identity in Christ and the gifts God has placed in them was life-giving. I don't think he knew what a handful I was when I first arrived. I was a fulltime job for an entire team of people, and a team of people is what I soon found surrounding me.

At first, I was extremely grateful for the attention and love of others. They were my biggest cheerleaders for my new life in Christ. People I didn't even know were trying to help me grow, and all I wanted to do was accommodate them. Amazingly, I went from not giving a "bleepty-bleep" what anyone thought of me to doing anything and everything I could do to please them.

Unbeknownst to me I was afflicted with the debilitating disease of *people pleasing*. This particular malady manifests a range of symptoms from mild to severe. The mild form is when the afflicted person wants a small circle of people— usually family, friends and those in leadership— to really like them. They will do just about anything to gain those people's approval. Those who suffer with a severe case of people pleasing want the **whole world** to LOVE them, and they will do whatever—I repeat, *whatever*—it takes to make this happen.

I wish I would have had just a mild case of this craziness, but no! I had to have the severe form of the disease. I was going fruit loops trying to change the person I was. I felt my church family could never love the old me, so I did all I could to be someone they would love. You can just imagine how vulnerable I was, trying to please almost 300 church members. I was overwhelmed.

In time, one thing became apparent. Although people were well-meaning, some were not completely led by the Lord in their efforts. I had become their "new project." They began telling me everything they had ever learned, *all at once.* Oh, they gave lots of great advice and constructive criticism. The problem was, they expected me to immediately make the changes they suggested.

One person told me I *had* to read this book. Another person told me I *had* to read that book. Some said I *had* to act this way, and some said I *had* to dress that way. For others, I *had* to be available to counsel on the phone 24/7, even though my children were very young and needed my attention. I *had* to do this, and I *had* to do that. Quite frankly, I had *had* it.

Please don't get me wrong. I am extremely grateful that someone...*anyone*...cared about me and wanted to help me grow for it was not a task for the weak of heart. Not everyone was demanding, and most of the people's input was great. It was just too much to take in and apply at one time. When I became increasingly frustrated, I should have stopped and prayed to God for *His* input.

Yes, I am slower than most people; it is true. When I finally reached my breaking point, I went down fast and hard. Looking back, I can see that God allowed me to experience a season of people pleasing so that I would turn totally to Him for my self-worth. He doesn't want us dependent on people; He wants us dependent on Him.

Scripture says, "Christ has set us free to live a free life. So take your stand! Never again let anyone put a harness of slavery on you" (Galatians 5:1 The Message). What a life-changing verse! Through this truth, I finally began to realize that I couldn't do everything that everyone requested and I didn't have to. I needed to work out *my* salvation with God. This is my prime "sweet spot"—in Him. And oh, how sweet He is!

GOD HAS A *CUSTOM* BUILD SHEET FOR YOU

Allen shared something else with me during our road trip to Colorado. He explained how all factory-made vehicles are built from a *standard* build sheet. The only time a vehicle has a *custom* build sheet is when extra bells and whistles are added. Even then its uniqueness is limited because the extras are picked from a uniform checklist.

You and I, on the other hand, were created by God as unique individuals. We each have a *custom* build sheet unique to us. No cookie cutters here. We are not stamped, punched or crafted from any mold that can be reused. Each one of us was created for a specific purpose and designed to carry a specific load. King David said it this way:

> **"Oh yes, you shaped me first inside, then out; you formed me in my mother's womb. I thank you, High God—you're breathtaking! Body and soul, I am marvelously made! I worship in adoration— what a creation! You know me inside and out, you know every bone in my body; you know exactly how I was made, bit by bit, how I was sculpted from nothing into something. Like an open book,**

you watched me grow from conception to birth; all the stages of my life were spread out before you, the days of my life all prepared before I'd even lived one day."

—Psalm 139:13-16 The Message

Wow! What an amazing truth. You and I are marvelously created by God and He knows *everything* about us. He knows how we are wired within and can see every stage and page of our life before it takes place. What an amazing God!

Understanding how you are wired comes through being in relationship with Him. Years ago, our pastor, Ed Shirrell, shared that as a young pastor he tried to glean wisdom from those with more experience than he had. He explained how on one occasion, while an older evangelist was visiting the church, he asked him, "In all your years of ministry, what would be the most helpful tip you could give a person?"

The evangelist answered, "Find out what God's will is for you and in what capacity he created you to function, and then function in it. Some people are like a cargo plane, a jumbo jet or a glider. Others are like an F-15 fighter, a sea plane or a helicopter. Each is designed for a specific task and payload. Finding out what God created you to be will remove a lot of frustration and bring more fulfillment to your life."

Taking this analogy and putting it in terms of motorcycles, some of us are like trikes with a trailer, equipped for long distance rides. Others are like dressers, super glides or choppers—made to be sleek and showy with no back seat for passengers. Some of us resemble sport bikes or crotch rockets as I call them that are built for speed. And others are more like dirt bikes or four-wheelers—rough and rugged, able to handle tough terrain.

Each style is made for different purposes and different capacities. As hard as it is for me to say, being the "Harley Girl" that I am, no one is better than another. They are just different.

As for me, some days I don't see myself like a motorcycle or an airplane. I see myself as a lawn chair with a bunch of helium balloons tied to it and some crazy bird trying to pop them. Have ya been there?

The fact is, in each season of our lives, we may resemble a different vehicle, depending on our function and the load we need to carry. For instance, when Allen and I were younger and had no children, we rode an old '51 panhead. It was a hardtail with a suicide clutch and jockey shift. There is no way I could ride that bike today.

Once we had our two girls, things changed. We went through a season in which we didn't own a motorcycle at all. During that time, I saw myself as the itty-bitty bicycle clowns ride in parades. I was pedaling as fast as I could, but I never got very far. Thankfully, God didn't leave me there. Seasons changed and He promoted me to a new ride. That's what He does throughout our lives. He evaluates our needs and gives us the equipment we need to get the job done. As the psalmist says,

"{*God*} satisfies your mouth [your necessity and desire at your personal age and situation]

with good so that your youth, renewed, is like the eagle's [strong, overcoming, soaring]!"

—Psalm 103:5 AMP
Italicized word in brackets added for clarity.

So what does your custom build sheet look like? In what way and for what purpose did God design *you*? It might change from season to season, but it doesn't change the fact that "Each person is given something to do that shows who God is" (1 Corinthians 12:7, The Message). Finding out what God created you to be will remove a lot of frustration and bring fulfillment to your life. This is your major "sweet spot" in which you were destined to find rest.

GOD WANTS YOU TO FIND REST FOR YOUR SOUL

I think you will agree that having peace and rest is priceless. Jesus gives us an awesome invitation to enter His rest in the Gospel of Matthew. He says,

"Come to me, all you who are weary and burdened, and I will give you rest. Take my yoke upon you and learn from me, for I am gentle and humble in heart, and you will find rest for your souls."

—Matthew 11:28-29 NIV

Carefully read the passage again. Did you notice Jesus said, "learn from me"? This means He wants us to spend time with Him in His Word and in prayer, learning how He lived. He is willing to teach, if we are willing to listen. When we allow Him to teach us who He really is, He will replace all the misconceptions we have of Him. As a result, we will become more and more confident in who He made us to be.

Once I began to understand my custom build sheet, I began to learn how to manage my new freedom in Christ. He set me free to be the best "me" I could be. Little by little, I began to notice more quickly when I was doing too much—that is, when I was doing things God had not asked me to do. You would think the problem was solved, right? Wrong! Recognizing over commitment is only the first step toward changing things. I also needed to take *action*. I needed to begin to *do* something different in order to get different results.

The immediate problem God revealed to me was my inability to say a special two-letter word. Do you know what that word is? It's **NO**. Let's practice saying it together. Ready, set "No!" Oh, come on. You can do better than that. Say it with me one more time…"**NO!**" Very good!

Over time and with lots of practice, I have learned to say no to the requests and opportunities that are not from God. Sometimes I will say out loud to whoever will listen, even if it's just me, "No, I cannot do that. I am not a jumbo jet! I am not equipped for that load at this point."

Now that I have accepted who God made me to be, knowing my gifts and abilities, I try to seek His will on the front end of opportunities. This helps head off any craziness before it starts. Isn't that a fresh idea? He has taught me not to commit to things right away but to pull away and pray. If I have *peace* in my heart, I move forward. If I don't have peace or there's confusion and strife about it, the answer is no. This is the life-changing principle of Colossians 3:15 (AMP):

"And let the peace (soul harmony which comes) from Christ rule (act as umpire continually) in your hearts [deciding and settling with finality all questions that arise in your minds, in that peaceful state] to which as [members of Christ's] one body you were also called [to live]...."

By reading God's Word for His wisdom and sitting under good, balanced teaching, you too can learn to hear God's voice. Saying yes, to what God says yes to and no, to what He says no to, is a major key to entering His rest. Besides, you don't want to be so busy doing "good" things that you are too exhausted to accept God's *best* when it comes your way. In God's best is where you find rest. What a priceless sweet spot!

You Can Trust His Timing

With each passing day, I am growing in a new confidence I have never had before. As I learn to hear God's voice and rest in His "custom plan" for my life, I rarely do what everyone else is doing. At first this was difficult and felt quite strange. There have been times I have even felt guilty or weird when I said no to someone or I didn't sign up to do something that everyone else seemed to be doing. But because my driving desire is for God's best, those feelings have waned.

Timing is so important. Ecclesiastes 3:1 in The Message says, "There's an opportune time to do things, a right time for everything on the earth." All the things I couldn't say no to were good, but they weren't necessarily good for me at the time. Doing the right thing at the right time is critical. Doing the right thing at the *wrong* time or too many things at once often creates chaos. Trust me…I know. I was going crazy and acting like a fool trying to satisfy everybody's wishes.

I remember a time when our youth pastor asked all the students and a number of adults to read the book *A Divine Revelation of Hell* by Mary K. Baxter. Before long, countless people started asking me, "Have you read the book yet? Have you started it? I'll loan it to you," or "I'll buy it for you." And when I told them no, I got the question that really surprised me: "Well why not?" It was as if I had missed the will of God and wasn't as "spiritual" as they were.

At that point in my Christian walk, I was well aware of the disease of people pleasing and did not want to be re-infected. As 1 Thessalonians 2:4 (NIV) says, "…We are not trying to please people but God, who tests our hearts." By God's grace, I held my ground and did not try to read the book at that time. About two years later, I felt the Lord wanted me to read it, so I did. I couldn't put it down. I cried through the whole thing with a repentant heart for those who are dying and going to hell without the real love, peace and joy that can only be found in Jesus. Again, *timing is critical.*

Please don't get me wrong. I am not encouraging you to purposely go against your leaders with a rebellious heart. It is good to be encouraged to read life-changing material, and we should be open to what our leaders are encouraging us to do. Ultimately, however, we have to follow what we believe God's plan is for us. We have to want to please Him more than we want to please others.

I encourage you to trust God's timing. He knows you and He knows what is best for you at your present age and stage of your life. If you pray about something and He gives you peace, proceed. If you pray and just can't seem to have a settled "thumbs-up" about it, stay put. God's plan, His ways and His timing are always best.

WHERE ARE *YOUR* SWEET SPOTS?

As you discover God's will for your life and who He has custom-designed you to be, you will also begin to discover sweet spots in many areas of your life. Stop and think about all the choices you are presented with every day. God's *best* choice for you is what you want, right? Well, begin to ask Him for his input. He has promised to give it to you. He says in His Word,

"Where is the man {*or woman*} who fears the Lord? God will teach him {*or her*} how to choose the best."

—Psalm 25:12 TLB
Italicized words in brackets added for clarity.

As you pray and involve God in your life, He will show you the best choice in each situation you face. You have His Word on it. Knowing God's best helps reveal your sweet spots. They include the church that's right for you, the job that's tailor-made for your skills, and the relationships you need to grow and mature.

One of the things I have prayed for over the years is divine connections. I want the Lord to hook me up with awesome sisters who are hungry for His best and have the godly qualities I lack. You can pray this too. It is a prayer you can be confident He will answer! It may take time, but He will always be faithful to provide you with just the right friends at just the right time.

Right now, my BFF is an answer to one of those prayers. What's funny is, our pastor tried to hook us up about ten years ago. He obviously saw a common connection we couldn't see at the time. We each had to go through some hard lessons in order to be ready for one another. That is the way it is sometimes. God has to get us ready to receive the blessing He has prepared for us. The truth is neither my friend nor I would have liked each other very much had we gotten close before it was God's timing. But now we share a sweet spot together.

Another sweet spot that I have discovered is the one I share with my husband on the back of our bike. It's not just any bike…it's a Harley and that's what it has to be for me! It's my little piece of heaven. No phones, TVs or computers. The kids and all the other demands of life are quieted. There my soul rests within me while we are cruising down the highway, listening to the most awesome sound ever created— loud pipes. Ahhh…they make me smile!

Believe it or not, most of this book has been conceived while sitting on the back seat of a bike over many years. Hence the subtitle, "Lessons from the Back Seat." There are about 700 people in our church now, and I don't think that many of them would say their sweet spot is on the back seat of a bike with loud pipes. If I would have kept trying to be like all of them, I would have never realized the joy of knowing God created me for this. No, it's not a substitute for going to church, but it is an awesome sweet spot.

What are your sweet spots? Invite God into your life and ask Him to reveal them. He will teach you how to choose the best and experience His rest.

DON'T LET ANYTHING KEEP YOU FROM FINDING YOURS

Just as sure as there is a God in heaven that loves you, there is an enemy on earth that hates you. Satan and his demonic forces are real, and they do not want you finding your sweet spots. They will use anything possible to deny and derail you from God's best.

I almost missed out on an awesome connection with my husband on our road trip to Colorado that day. I was full of fear from my past—fear of being rejected, laughed at, misunderstood and hurt again by him. In the past, I would have accepted the fear and withdrew into a cocoon of insecurity. But by God's grace, I looked fear in the face and defeated it.

By not caving into my fears and choosing to trust God, I was blessed in an amazing way—a way I would not have dreamed possible not too long ago. I gave Allen a chance to be the new creation God was helping him to be; to ask questions and share his insights. As a result, we found a new sweet spot together as a couple. This is God's plan for marriages—for husbands and wives to function together in harmony as one.

When we allow ourselves to be tweaked individually by our Maker, we can become one together without spark knocking and backfiring. Yes, you may need more frequent tune-ups than others, but that's okay. Remember that it's *your* sweet spot, not someone else's.

The bottom line of this lesson: The only one who can find your sweet spots is **you**. No one else can do it for you. You don't need to find sister "So-and-So's" sweet spot or your BFF's sweet spot or even your man's sweet spot. You need to find yours. Sure, you can follow the good examples of others in the areas of study, true discipleship, dedication and perseverance. But ultimately, you have to walk with God and discover His specific will for your life.

Lesson Summary

<u>Something to Hold On To</u>

We are a work in progress, from before we are born to the end of our days. The Lord is continually building us. He gives us tune ups, recalibrates us and promotes us as we trade in the "same old, same old" for something new. We don't need to please people, just Him. He is faithful to give us the equipment we need when we need it to carry our loads. As we line ourselves up with our Creator's perfect will, we will find freedom to ride in our groove, functioning in the heavenly *sweet spots* He created just for us!

<u>Rena's playlist:</u>

- "Free To Be Me" ~ by Francesca Battistelli

- "Brave" ~ by Nichole Nordeman

- "Freedom" ~ by Darrell Evans

- "I Love Your Presence" ~ by Vineyard Music

Questions for personal or group reflection:

- You are one of a kind, created by God for a specific purpose. How would you describe your custom design—with what kind of bike would you compare yourself? Why?

- In your own words, describe what _people pleasing_ is. Are you dealing with any of its symptoms? If so, which ones? Why is this dangerous to your spiritual health?

- What is a good rule of thumb for committing or not committing to something? (Check out Colossians 3:15 for some help.) Is there anything right now you need to say no to?

- Name some of the _sweet spots_ in your life. Invite God into your life and ask Him to reveal them. He will teach you how to choose the best and experience His rest.

- What is your greatest "take away" from this lesson—what came alive and jumped off the pages that you want to remember?

---

[1]_Retrieved from Facebook._

"A truly good friend will openly correct you. You can trust a friend who corrects you, but kisses from an enemy are nothing but lies."

—King Solomon
Proverbs 27:5-6 CEV

You've Got 'em…
I've Got 'em…
Everybody's Got 'em!

"This is what the Lord says—your Redeemer, the Holy One of Israel: 'I am the Lord your God, who teaches you what is good for you and leads you along the paths you should follow.'"

Isaiah 48:17 NLT

One beautiful afternoon my hubby and I were on our way to meet up with some friends. They were waiting for us about 20 minutes away on the side of the road so we could then "peel out" together to an event. We were running late, and if we didn't get on it, we would miss them.

As we were moving from a two-lane road to a four-lane highway, I gave my man some much needed direction. Knowing we would be exiting soon and were in the wrong lane, I engaged in the "fine art" of backseat driving. It is *fine*, but there is an art to it!

At that time, our pipes were nice and loud. So I poked him in the ribs and yelled, "Hey! Aren't we taking Highway 21?" The only reply I received was the sound of the engine revving as he pulled in the clutch and downshifted, nothing more. He was so cool and he knew it!

The truth is, he stayed in the lane we were in because he could see something I could not. Eventually, he slowed down to change lanes, and we fell in place behind a truck. Now this wasn't just any truck. It was a *honking big* truck pulling a *honking big* boat.

After seeing the size of the rig, I was in shock that it was completely hidden from my view. My mouth hung wide open in amazement, and my chin nearly hit the pavement. Had I been the one in the front seat, I would have definitely eaten some bugs.

From my vantage point behind Allen, I couldn't see a single inch of the obstacle blocking us from where we needed to be. Looking back, I'm so glad Allen saw what I could not see and did what I would not have done. We would have been road jam for sure had we done what *I* thought was right.

That's when the Lord dropped this lesson into my spirit.

You've got 'em… I've got 'em… Everybody's got 'em! Whether we're young or old, male or female, rich or poor, smart or not so smart, we each have snares that affect us equally. They are called **blind spots**—areas in our lives we have been "blessed" with in which we simply cannot see. You know, the things you see in your husband and family members that they're oblivious to. The things your family and friends see in you, but are terrified to tell you for fear of being severely wounded. In this there is a definite lesson to be learned.

I Was Blind but I Didn't Know It

As I mentioned in Lesson 1, my parents split up when I was nine. At that time my mom had to go to work, holding up to three jobs to support us. That meant we got ourselves ready each morning and put ourselves on the bus. I began fixing my own hair, but I only fixed the parts I could see in the mirror. I simply didn't think about the back of my head because I couldn't see it.

One night when I was about eleven I returned home drunk and stoned from smoking pot. As weird as it may seem, I decided to cut my hair. I had been cutting my hair for quite some time and I was even cutting my mom's bangs. But I don't know what I was thinking that night.

When I woke up the next morning, my fairly long hair was gone on one side. Being a school day, I did the best I could to fix it. I put my hair in a ponytail, all but the part that didn't make it into the rubber band and I went on my way, acting like nothing was wrong.

Interestingly, Jesus said this is how some people act, declaring, "You say, 'I am rich; I have acquired wealth and do not need a thing.' But you do not realize that you are wretched, pitiful, poor, **blind** and naked" (Revelation 3:17 NIV).

I knew something was wrong with the back of my hair, but I didn't know how to fix it. I certainly wasn't going to draw attention to it. So I did the only thing I knew to do—I ignored it. I acted as if I was in need of nothing. I can't tell you how long I left my hair that way, but it was longer than a girl should. The sad thing is, I continued to live my life in the same way.

I don't know why no one took time to teach me how to use a hand mirror to see the back of my head. Most people probably thought my mom had taught me, but she hadn't. Life had changed really fast for us. Because my dad only gave her two weeks' notice before he left, one day she was fixing my hair, and the next day she barely had time to fix her own before she had to leave for work.

We shouldn't assume someone who has a problem has been taught how to fix it—even something simple. Nor should we judge them. We don't know their circumstances. Thank God somewhere along the way someone cared enough about me to help me deal with the rat's nest on the back of my head. They showed me my blind spot and taught me how to take care of it.

IDENTIFYING THE ULTIMATE BLIND SPOT

For some of us our blind spot is simply that we have yet to realize God loves and accepts us just the way we are—period. There is nothing we can do to cause Him to love us any more or less than He does. The Scripture says,

> "{*Jesus*} didn't, and doesn't, wait for us to get ready. He presented himself for this sacrificial death when we were far too weak and rebellious to do anything to get ourselves ready. And even if we hadn't been so weak, we wouldn't have known what to do anyway. But God shows and clearly proves His [own] love for us by the fact that while we were still sinners, Christ (the Messiah, the Anointed One) died for us."
>
> —Romans 5:6, 8

The Message and Amplified respectively; italicized word in brackets added for clarity.

The ultimate blind spot anyone can have is the one between us and God. It is one we must each come to grips with and work through. We can't be good enough to come to Him. We just have to come. That's all He wants. God reconnects us in relationship with Himself through what Jesus did on the cross. Wow! What amazing love!

It took me a ridiculously long time to get to the place where I knew God loved *me* just as I am. I fought this truth fiercely, thinking there was no way it could be that easy. By not accepting His unearnable and undeservable free gift of grace, I made my life harder than it needed to be. Thank God I'm finally beyond that point!

Ultimately, God wants us to reach the place of living in His grace. When He shows us a blind spot, He wants us to accept His correction and cooperate with Him to change it. For example, if He reveals an issue of anger or an unwillingness to forgive someone, both of which I have had to deal with, He wants us to run *to* Him, not *from* Him. In this mature stage of growth we learn to rest in His everlasting arms while He works out those things within us.

However, the truth is many of us have a hard time accepting God's correction. As Joyce Meyer says, we tend to *struggle* with God instead of *snuggle* with God. We kick and scream our way through many blind spot removal surgeries. We fight with Him until we are utterly exhausted. Eventually, we come back to the realization that He truly knows what's best, and we surrender to Him—that is, until the next blind spot is revealed. Then the process starts all over again.

Although I have been more of a kicker and screamer in the past, I have also been mature and cooperated with God's correction. Once I learned to accept His unconditional love, I needed to accept another major truth: Although God loves me as I am, He doesn't want me to stay that way. He wants me to cooperate with the work of His Holy Spirit to become like Jesus. The same is true for you.

I knew I was in need of change—a lot of change. A few delicate tweaks here and there were not going to get the job done. I needed a major overhaul! No one could better tell you how bad of a sinner I was or how much yuck was inside of me than me.

But I wanted my transformation to take place on *my* terms. I wanted all the dirty details of my life to remain between God and me and just a few others I chose to share it with. Although my transformation started this way, God eventually chose to change things up.

GROWING UP *HIS* WAY

God began to work deeply in me, and boy was I uncomfortable! He seemed to be stepping on my toes at every turn. As I read my Bible in private, the Holy Spirit began showing me things about my character that I had never seen. There were attitudes and actions that needed to change. If that wasn't bad enough, He began to do the same thing to me in public during our church services. He spoke to me through my pastor, visiting evangelists and even Sunday school teachers. Little by little, He was revealing my blind spots in an effort to bring change to my life.

When I first surrendered myself to God, I really dug the messages. They were all about His love for me, and they made me feel so good inside. Sermons that don't require much effort from the hearers are considerably more pleasant to receive. However, they produce little or no change. They lack the ability to cause us to look intently in our own heart. As a result, we remain spiritual babies.

Like any good parent, God wants us to grow up. Through the apostle Peter, He instructs us to...

"Get rid of all evil behavior. Be done with all deceit, hypocrisy, jealousy, and all unkind speech. Like newborn babies, you must crave pure spiritual

milk so that you will grow into a full experience of salvation. Cry out for this nourishment, now that you have had a taste of the Lord's kindness."

—1 Peter 2:1-3 NLT

In the process of maturing us, our Father often uses gentle whispers to get our attention and bring correction to our lives. If that doesn't work, He uses "kid gloves," giving us a little jab here and there to set us straight. And for those like me, who are hard headed, He gives a good whack with a spiritual two-by-four to move us in the right direction.

Except for God's gentle whisper, none of these methods of correction are what I would call *fun*. But they do get our attention. Being the stubborn girl that I am, I've been whacked more times than I can count or want to admit. I have broken out in a cold sweat many times during a sermon, fighting the urge to run from the conviction of the Holy Spirit. But when I yield to His promptings, He softens my heart so He can work in and through me. I usually end up crying in front of God and everyone else, and it's not just a sniffle. We're talking about a full-blown, blubbering cry.

Why does our heavenly Father correct us? Why does He reveal our blind spots? It's not to be mean as some might think. His only goal is to help us. We are His children, and He wants us to learn who He is, who we are in Him, and then grow. Just like we use different methods to teach our children, He uses different methods to teach us, knowing and doing only what's best. He says in His Word,

"'For I know the plans I have for you,' declares the Lord, 'plans to prosper you and not to harm you, plans to give you hope and a future.'"

—Jeremiah 29:11 NIV

From the start, I've had a deep desire to grow spiritually and emotionally. I have pleaded with God to change me many times. With a broken and apologetic heart, I've cried out for Him to make me into someone who would bring honor and glory to His name. Somewhere along the way, however, I lost sight of this request. As a result, I felt sucker punched by His discipline, when all He was doing was answering my prayers.

Sometimes I picture God sitting on His throne looking down at me with His elbows on His knees and His chin in His hands saying, "You're the one who prayed all those 'big girl' prayers, right? Well, I'm giving you your 'big girl' answers. I'm helping you change to bring Me glory."

Initially, I wanted to kick myself in the butt for praying those prayers. But now I wouldn't take back a single one or change one painful thing I've been through. I have learned so much and have gotten closer to being more like Jesus in the process.

Have you struggled with God's correction? Have you thought of God as a "big jerk" because of all the difficulty you have experienced, when in fact the difficulties He has allowed in your life are actually an answer to your prayers? Give it some time. Don't run away. Surrender yourself to Him. There will come a day when you will be glad you prayed!

WORD UP!

One of the biggest tools God uses to reveal our blind spots and mature us is His Word. Regardless of what others may say, only God's Word in the hands of His Holy Spirit has the power to change us. Ladies, God's Word is **for us**, not against us! It is to help us, not hurt us. I don't know about you, but I need *all* the help I can get. We are told that...

"All Scripture is God-breathed and is useful for teaching, rebuking, correcting and training in righteousness, so that the man {*and woman*} of God may be thoroughly equipped for every good work."

—2 Timothy 3:16-17 NIV

Italicized word in brackets added for clarity.

You and I need to be taught, corrected and trained in righteousness, which is right living. We also need to be *rebuked*, which basically means "to be reprimanded, called down, or called on the carpet."

After many years of doing the kicking and screaming thing, I now *want* God to correct me when I'm wrong, and I want Him to do it quickly. I don't want to go around acting like a fool one minute more than I have to. And since I prefer my corrections to also be gentle, I try hard not to fight with my Daddy God anymore. Again, He has a *good* plan for you and me and knows what's best.

God's Word is His basic plan for our lives. It is "...alive and powerful. It is sharper than the sharpest two-edged sword, cutting between soul and spirit, between joint and marrow. It exposes our innermost thoughts and desires" (Hebrews 4:12

NLT). Once we learn that God's Word is meant to help us grow up, we won't be caught off guard when correction comes. Trust me—it's going to come!

My heart for us is that we will not run from God's truth, but submit to it. If it is truly our desire to be more like Jesus and for God to help us be humble like He is, then the sooner we allow His Word to work in us and not fight it, the better off we'll be.

Remember, you and I cannot transform our minds on our own. I've tried it and it doesn't work. Only God can transform our minds and hearts through His Word! So read it. Study it. Memorize it. He can and will transform your life IF you let Him.

"Therefore, I urge you, brothers and sisters, in view of God's mercy, to offer your bodies as a living sacrifice, holy and pleasing to God—this is your true and proper worship. Do not conform to the pattern of this world, but be transformed by the renewing of your mind. Then you will be able to test and approve what God's will is—his good, pleasing and perfect will."

—Romans 12:1-2 NIV

Taking It Like a Big Girl

As I mentioned at the opening, God uses people in our lives to show us our blind spots. Because of the negative and unhealthy correction I experienced in my past, receiving correction from others has often been tough. It used to make me nauseous when someone revealed a fault—as if my insides were being ripped out. It still does at times.

On top of that, receiving correction sometimes causes the "old me" to rise up and try to defend myself. It's the part of me that is prideful and thinks "I am all that and a bag of chips." Thankfully, I have learned to go to the Lord in prayer. In His presence I'm reminded that I'm *not* all that or even close. It's in those times when we come face to face with our shortcomings and wrong attitudes that God's unconditional love as a **GOOD** Father shines brightly.

Not too long ago I could tell that something was wrong in my relationship with a friend of mine. I felt like there was a wall between us being reinforced with heavy-duty rebar. As it became more apparent, I began to pray. I wanted to be sure it was not my imagination or Satan, the "accuser of the brethren," coming to bring division between us. When things didn't change, I began to really grieve over our relationship.

One day, this friend called me out of the blue. She said God had given her a dream and in it, He had shown her that I was grieving over our friendship. *He's so cool like that!* She then asked me if I would like to ride with her to run some errands so that we could talk. I agreed and made the needed arrangements.

Initially, I was happy for the opportunity to fix whatever I had done to cause the rift. However, my happiness quickly changed into thoughts of defending myself—even though I didn't know what the issue was. The old me would have just drank another one, said a few choice words, and blown the relationship off, saying a few more choice words. I went through a lot of friends that way. It's an old survival instinct that still dogs me every now and then. But God wouldn't let me run. Instead, He put it in my heart to do the right thing—to face correction with His grace.

When the day of truth came, I drove to my friend's house, praying the whole way. It was only by God's grace that I made it to her house at all that day. He gave me the strength to whip my old nature's impulse to turn around and drive home.

Before we left to do her errands, we prayed together for God to be glorified in our conversation and fellowship. You see, we both have a heart for God and didn't want to do anything to cause pain to the other. Soon the issue that had been festering became clear and could be dealt with. I had recently made some decisions that my friend was concerned about. She knew of my past struggles and thought I had made some wrong choices.

Right then and there I could have said, "That's none of yo' 'bidness!" But that would have only shut down communication and possibly severe our friendship for good. The truth is she was right! Even though it was not all exactly the way she viewed it, I could see where she was coming from. While agreeing with her on why she could come to her conclusions, I carefully and gently, **not** defensively, explained the reasons for my actions. She received my explanation, and I received her correction. With God's help I am working to make the necessary changes so that a misunderstanding like that won't happen again.

This was really a HUGE deal for me. In a way, I had gotten too big for my britches, and my friend helped me see it. I am so glad she cared enough to *speak the truth in love* to me that day. She could have totally crushed me had she decided to react to her first thoughts and been quick to confront me, but she didn't. She told me that she purposefully prayed, sought God's heart, and searched her own in order to know what she needed to say before we talked.

That's something I can respect and learn from. If the Lord chooses to use her again in my life or we end up working together in a mutual situation, I won't have any problem listening to and respecting what she has to say.

Thank God I'm growing! I am learning to receive correction and not take it personally. I am realizing that even though I sometimes disappoint those who are close to me and they point it out, they still love me. It is for my good, and they are helping me grow to the next level. God's way always works best.

We Each Have a Part to Play

Okay...so what if my friend had said "No" to God after He gave her that dream? She could have easily said, "So what if Rena is grieving. It's no big deal. I'm *not* doing it, God!" I'm sure it was just as hard for her as it was for me to deal with the situation. I am so very thankful that she obeyed God. She helped me to mature and become *healthy and full of love* as God intends.

That is one of the main functions of the body of Christ. God has given us apostles, prophets, evangelists, pastors and teachers to unify our faith, equip us to do His work and build up His church. He says,

> **"Then** *we will no longer be immature like children.* **We won't be tossed and blown about by every wind of new teaching. We will not be influenced when people try to trick us with lies so clever they sound like the truth. Instead,** *we will speak the truth in love,* **growing in every way more and more like Christ, who is the head of his body, the church. He makes the whole body fit together perfectly. As each**

part does its own special work, it helps the other parts grow, so that the whole body is healthy and growing and full of love."

—Ephesians 4:14-16 NLT
Emphasis added

Some of you may be thinking, as I'm sometimes tempted to think, *Oh, No! Not me! I'm not gonna let anyone tell me anything. And I'm sure not gonna tell anyone else anything either.* But that way of thinking is wrong. We each have a part to play in God's work.

The truth is we will always have people bringing correction to our lives: our parents, teachers, bosses, friends, and don't forget our darling hubbies who come with all those in-laws! If that's not enough, even our children will start telling us things once they reach a certain age.

I have many regrets in this area. First, I regret not being able to listen to my husband more. Too often I saw Allen as my enemy instead of my friend. The most damaging part of this is that it was a bad example for our daughters. My second regret is that I didn't let my daughters practice on me more and bring me correction when they were younger. I could have better equipped them in giving and receiving correction to help others. Sadly, I didn't know enough at the time to receive their input as often as I should have in a constructive way.

As wives and mothers in the body of Christ, one of our roles is to help our own families learn and grow in God's ways. But we can't help others learn what we ourselves have not learned. Once we learn it, then we have the ability and responsibility to share it with others.

GIVING CORRECTION...THE RIGHT WAY

Thank God I have grown over the years, and I am getting new opportunities to listen to my daughters and Allen, my awesome friend. I have also been blessed to walk with them through some tough things they have faced in their own lives. Which brings us to the flipside of receiving correction and that's *giving correction*. Again, we each have a part to play in learning our blind spots.

Now ladies, this is not a license to go looking for things in others that you think they should deal with. We all have more than enough stuff of our own to keep us busy. God does not need us going around magnifying and pointing out peoples' issues like crazy vigilantes.

I would say that about 99 percent of the time, God is dealing with *my* issues and heart. When He shows me something in someone else, it's almost always so that I will pray for them. Sometimes, I get to speak into their lives and it is usually when I would rather keep my mouth shut.

Honestly, I don't want to do more than God desires and neither should you. The last thing we want to do is make matters worse. So, if you are to say something to someone, pray first. Ask God to help you *know that you know* He wants to use you to help Him *help* them. The key word here is **HELP.**

You should also pray to have the right words, attitude and motives. Remember, only God can give a person the power to change. We are to speak the truth in love. What they do with the insight He gives us to share is not our responsibility, but *how we share* it is. It may be the truth, but if it's not spoken in the right way, at the right time, and with the right motives, it will do the opposite of what God intends. Truth spoken in the right way, at the right time, with the right motives, produces the right results—godly change.

It's "Soul" Good!

Over the past twenty years I have seen correction given in awesome ways that brought God glory. I have also seen it done in ways that caused Him grief and an undesired outcome. I have seen people on the receiving end accept God's grace when a blind spot was revealed, making the needed adjustments. I have also seen people reject His grace, and it was not a pretty thing.

This knowledge causes me to pray and seek God all the more when someone points out a blind spot in me or when He chooses to trust me with someone else's. I am convinced that the healing I have received in my soul—which is our mind, will and emotions—would never have taken place had I not submitted to the Lord's correction along the way.

I am overflowing with love and gratefulness for every man and woman of God He has placed in my life. They are the ones who have done the hard work, allowing God to bring correction in them first, then in me. They have helped me "...grow in the grace and knowledge of our Lord..." (2 Peter 3:18 NLT). I'm the woman I am today because of their example, sacrifice and many prayers.

Interestingly, I didn't pick any of these dear ones—God did. We don't get to choose who He uses in our lives. That may seem like a drag, but God knows exactly who we need to speak to us. I needed a truckload of people for several years. He didn't always bring me someone I knew and loved. Many times it was someone I had never met, and sometimes it was a person I was not very fond of. But I reckon He can do it how He wants. He is God, ya know!

It's definitely easier said than done to give up your right to control this part of your ride with Jesus. I understand. I had to learn to trust God and grow in this area just like you will. As we submit first to Him and then to one another, we will all grow with each passing experience. The important thing is keeping a heart attitude of wanting God's best for everyone involved.

You can be sure, regardless of who God chooses, whether someone new to the responsibility of bringing correction or a practiced and skilled instructor of God's people, it will be for the good of your soul.

Chapter Summary

<u>Something to Hold On To</u>

On the bike that day, Allen saw what I couldn't see, and he did what needed to be done to keep us safe. But he first had to deal with what was in my blind spot. It was only after that he was able to make the necessary lane changes that put us into position to reach our destination.

Let God be the One in the front seat. He's so much more capable of driving your life than you are. He sees everything ahead and all of the obstacles keeping you from reaching your destinations. Let Him help you see the blind spots in your soul—let Him use who He wants to use to reveal and heal your life. In the process, He will use you to help others see their blind spots so they can get where they need to be. Ultimately, His goal is to restore your soul so that you can in turn help to restore someone else's.

Rena's playlist:

- "The Motions" ~ by Matthew West

- "Twenty-Four" ~ by Switchfoot

- "Learning to Be the Light" ~ by Newworldsong

Questions for personal or group reflection:

- Name some of the *blind spots* God has revealed to you. Who has He used to help reveal them? How does He want you to respond to this revelation?

- Why does your heavenly Father correct you—what are His purposes and goals? (Check out Hebrews 12:5-13.)

- How important is God's Word to your spiritual growth? What is it designed to do? (Check out 2 Timothy 3:16-17; Hebrews 4:12; Romans 12:1-2; James 1:21.)

- Sometimes God will use you to reveal someone else's blind spot. Explain the right way of giving correction. What should your ultimate motive be?

- What is your greatest "take away" from this lesson— what came alive and jumped off the pages that you want to remember?

"The Bible reveals that a wife's respect for her husband is as powerful as her husband's love is to her. This is why Ephesians 5:33 says what it says. A husband needs to feel respect for who he is in the same way a wife needs to feel love for who she is. When a husband's need for respect is met, he responds. ...Though a husband may not deserve respect and a wife may not feel any respect, contemptuous speech never touches the human spirit in a positive and lasting manner."

—Dr. Emerson Eggerichs[1]

"Lord, Don't Let Me Be a Drip On My Husband's Trip!"

A good woman is hard to find, and worth far more than diamonds.

Proverbs 31:10 The Message

Our road trip to Rocky Mountain National Park, Colorado was one in which I learned many lessons. Of all the journeys we had taken, this one was extra special. It was our first big trip without our children, and we were pumped! Allen had been dreaming of this for years.

We had just finished finalizing the details when Allen came home from work one day with a serious look on his face. As he rubbed his neck, he told me he needed to go to the doctor. Now, you have to know my husband. He *never* does this. In fact, he doesn't care for doctors at all. Prior to this, I could count on one hand the number of times he had seen a doctor in the previous twenty-five years. Whatever was bothering him was serious.

Not thinking, I started to tease him. I quickly saw that this time was different. I recalibrated my focus and asked, "What's going on, babe?"

He told me that while he was checking through his beard for ticks after working outside the previous day, he found a lump on his neck. I reached out and felt the lump myself. One of his lymph nodes was as big as an extra-large egg and hard as a rock.

I tried to downplay it saying, "Oh, it's probably just an infection that has settled in your lymph node. It's probably no big deal. Maybe a tick did bite you while you were working outside." But in my gut, even I was not persuaded. We quickly made an appointment with the doctor for the next day.

After Allen was examined, the doctor gave him a prescription for antibiotics. He told us that if there was no change by the end of the medication, which was about two weeks, he wanted the lymph node to come out. When we told him about our upcoming vacation plans, he encouraged us to go. But he made us promise to come back and see him as soon as we returned.

We continued with our daily routines and maintained business as usual until our vacation. Little did I know the adventurous time of testing that was ahead.

God Answers Unselfish Prayers

When the doctor found no other swollen lymph nodes, I was not happy. As the doctor and I exchanged a brief glance at one another, I knew he wasn't either. Neither of us told Allen our concern. As fear and worry tried to take me captive, I cried out to God for help, and His peace began to comfort me.

We confided briefly in a few friends and our pastor for prayer. One of the places I gained support was from my Bible study group that met once a month. We called ourselves "The Sister Chicks." Like good sisters, we would love, support, listen to, and pray for one another, even holding each other's hand when needed.

One evening when it came time to share prayers and praises, I mentioned what was going on with Allen. I told them what the doctor had said and about our vacation that was almost upon us. I also shared that with two neck surgeries under my belt and a problem I had sitting on our bike for very long, I was afraid of experiencing physical pain during our trip. My reason: I truly didn't want to be crabby with Allen because I was in pain or because I was too doped up on medication.

I tried to tie things up neatly by concluding my request with, "Please pray that I won't be a drip on my husband's trip." This expression came to me from the book of Proverbs, which says,

"A nagging spouse is like the drip, drip, drip of a leaky faucet; you can't turn it off, and you can't get away from it."

— Proverbs 27:15-16 The Message

I had read this verse many times before, but I seldom saw myself as *that* spouse. It just never dawned on me, thinking I was better than that. Oh, but the Holy Spirit, who lives in me, knew it was me to a tee. He brought this truth from scripture back to my remembrance exactly when I needed to hear it.

This may come as a shock, but this kind of unselfish prayer request concerning a situation with my husband was rare for me. Knowing deep down what we might be facing with his health, I sincerely wanted his dream vacation to be everything he needed it to be. In my heart, I knew this was possibly Allen's last big trip, and for the first time it needed to be *all about him*!

God answered my unselfish request in a big way. Our vacation was truly the best we had ever had. The time we spent together playing in the mountains on our bike could not have been more perfect. When it was all said and done, I had no regrets. God helped me to not be a drip on my husband's trip.

Are You a Nagger or a Ragger?

Let me back the bus up and say that when I first asked my friends to pray for me, we all shared a giggle. Only it was that uncomfortable giggle we let out when we can relate to a behavior that's not so good. They all knew exactly where I was coming from. As women, we all have the capability to nag and rag our husbands. Some of us just do it more easily and more often than others.

God had been *trying* to deal with me about my attitude toward my husband for years. I had a tendency to both rag and nag him 24/7. I was constantly on his butt about something. After camping out way too long in "harass county," I finally began to feel the conviction of God's Spirit.

Mind you, when He first started dealing with me about this I still didn't think I was *that* kind of wife. How easily we can convince ourselves issues such as these don't pertain to us. As in the previous lesson, this was surely one of my blind spots.

My attitude initially got better when we started going to church. God began to tug at my heart, and I responded by making some changes here and there. Slowly but surely, He began shaping me into His image.

Unfortunately, when I began to experience constant physical pain and be on mega doses of medication, I reverted back to my old ways. I missed a lot of church services and became disconnected from the body of Christ. Like a severed limb separated from its life source, I was beginning to die spiritually.

Thank God, He didn't leave me in my mess. In His great love for me, as we learned in Lesson 3, He brought discipline and correction my way. One of those spiritual 2x4s hit me during our "end of spring fling" ride through the Grand Canyon of the Ozarks in Arkansas. I was maxing and relaxing, enjoying the scenery when I suddenly saw this cute little blue house sitting high and proud on a hill overlooking a valley. Instead of shutters covering the windows, it had large wooden hearts, and rebel flags hung as curtains.

I don't have anything against rebel flags per se. I have a great respect for southern pride, seeing that my momma's side of the family came from Alabama and many of them still live there. It's what the flag has come to represent that bothers me. To me, they represent hatred and rebellion, things that break God's heart.

You can imagine how much it grieved me when God showed me that the house represented me. On the outside, I was cute and lovely, but on the inside I stood tall with a spirit of rebellious pride and a form of hatred toward others, mostly men—especially my husband.

I was reminded of Jesus' words,

"A good person produces good things from the treasury of a good heart, and an evil person produces evil things from the treasury of an evil heart. What you say flows from what is in your heart."

—Luke 6:45 NLT

God was right! The words of my mouth revealed the true condition of my heart, and it wasn't pretty. No matter how hard I tried to completely love my husband, I eventually came back to the place where I subconsciously saw him as my enemy. As a result, I had little to no respect for him. But that was about to change.

To Respect or Not to Respect... That Is the Question

Emotional and physical abuse in my past was a major hindrance in my walk with God and relationship with others—and again, especially Allen. I had no respect for him, myself or anyone else when I came to Christ. This caused me to have an extremely hard time receiving correction. It also made being questioned intolerable. As you may recall from the previous lessons, I felt it was an intrusion into my business, something I guarded closely.

Ingredients like these do not make for a good marriage. They are the recipe for divorce—something I was all too familiar with. But I wholeheartedly *wanted* to respect my husband and obey the Lord and His Word. I had no clue of the battle I was in for.

I learned what the Bible says wives should do in Ephesians 5:33 (AMP):

"...Let the wife see that she respects *and* reverences her husband [that she notices him, regards him, honors him, prefers him, venerates, and

esteems him; and that she defers to him, praises him, and loves and admires him exceedingly]."

Up until this time, I had not known any woman who truly respected her husband. Those that had an appearance of respect did things behind their husbands' backs. I *knew* that wasn't respect. And I definitely wanted no part of what other women believed respect was; they seemed to be slowly dying as they lay down under the "lordship" of their husband. These examples left a lot to be desired.

I also didn't have a good example of respect from my parents who divorced when I was young. Unfortunately, this lack of respect and honor had been passed down from generation to generation. This is what King Ahasuerus', also known as King Xerxes, wise men warned him would happen if he did nothing in retaliation for Queen Vashti's open disrespect. She dishonored the King by refusing to join him at a banquet as he requested. The wise counselors knew this behavior would be reproduced in the women who heard of it. You can read the full story in Esther 1:10-21.

Clearly, I had many misconceptions of respect modeled before me, and as a result, I learned what *not* to do. But, I had the whole thing completely wrong, just as Queen Vashti did. She and I both believed that the people we were supposed to respect had to *earn* it by behaving respectably, but that is not true. By believing this lie, we have perpetuated it and not only hurt our men, but also our daughters.

Yes, it is definitely easier to respect someone who behaves in a way worthy of respect. But that is only the **minimum** God requires of us. The law of God's grace requires us to go the extra mile in our relationships, even more so when someone is undeserving of our efforts. As Disciples of Christ, we are to do the right thing, even when we don't feel like it. We are to *act our way into a feeling*, not feel our way into an action. We are called to respect the position of our husbands and those in authority regardless of what they do. God makes this clear through Peter:

"Respect everyone, and love your Christian brothers and sisters. Fear God, and respect the king."

—1 Peter 2:17 NLT

So the question remains: to respect or not to respect? The choice is ours, as it always has been. But here is where the rubber meets the road, ladies. We will either be *doers* of the Word in this area of our marriages or not. It is the doers who are blessed. Those who hear only and choose not to obey deceive themselves right out of God's blessing (see James 1:22-25). This is where the Lord got my attention. I could not continue in my sin. I made the choice to respect, a choice I have to make daily. I am so grateful He loves me enough to teach me His ways.

You Want Me to Do *What*?

There's another instruction women tend to choke on, and that is to *submit* to their husbands. The thought of submitting has been and still is a joke to most ladies, even in the church. Just like the issue of respect, we have gotten mixed up about what true submission is.

I remember early in my walk with the Lord, there was a friend of mine who had finally met the man of her dreams. She was about to get married, and for her bridal shower I wrote the words *submit, submit, submit* all around the outer edge of her card. As she read it aloud at her church bridal shower, everyone laughed hysterically, verifying the value we women have placed on submission.

What does God's Word say?

"And further, submit to one another out of reverence for Christ. For wives, this means submit to your husbands as to the Lord. For a husband is the head of his wife as Christ is the head of the church. He is the Savior of his body, the church. As the church submits to Christ, so you wives should submit to your husbands in everything."

—Ephesians 5:21-24 NLT

My husband is a grace gift from God and probably the *only* man who would ever put up with me. However, because of my past and the fact that he is a man, deep down I did not trust him at all. And I truly believe trust is at the heart of the issue of submission. When we lack trust, we lack the ability to submit.

As you may recall, in lesson 1, "Rock My World...Please!" I vowed as a young teenager to never again need anyone to take care of me—especially a man. My lack of trust in people, including Allen, was rooted in that vow.

I met Allen at age fifteen, and by the time we began going to church, we had shared many crazy sin filled years together.

The things we did before accepting Christ only added to the wounds already in my heart and soul from childhood. This includes, but is not limited to, the abortion we had when I was eighteen.

Basically he gave me an ultimatum, "me or the baby." Along with his words, I had the words of Planned Parenthood ringing in my ears, "Do the easy thing and get rid of the blob of flesh," as they described it. With *no* encouragement to keep our baby, I chose to kill it. If I had known then what I know now, I would have chosen life—especially after feeling the life of each of our two girls within me as I carried them to term.

Recovering from the guilt and shame of my sins was a long and hard process. I now rest in God's promise to forgive our sins when we confess them (see 1 John 1:9). Thankfully, I can say the process is complete. With the help of many people's prayers, including one mighty woman of God, Beverly Kuenzle, the former director of the Pregnancy Care Center in our area, I am healed and free.

If you have had an abortion, please hear my heart: Do not waste one more minute hating yourself or holding those involved hostage with your unwillingness to forgive. Don't be afraid to face it and work through it. You may think it is not a problem, but I assure you it has wounded your soul and affects your life in ways you may not know. There's a "Mrs. Beverly" near you just like there was for me. Find her. She will not judge you; she will hold your hand while you find and receive God's grace and forgiveness.

Accepting His forgiveness where it is needed will produce an attitude of gratitude within you. From that attitude of gratitude, joy will begin to overflow from deep within your soul, and "...the joy of the Lord is your strength" (Nehemiah 8:10 NLT). God's joy will help you abound in love toward others, including your husband. Even if at first your submission is only because the Word says to, in time your faithful God will turn this around for the good of you both.

TRUE SUBMISSION
COMES FROM A STRONG POSITION

Personally, I have struggled with submission just as much, if not more, than respect. For a long time I felt both were to be given from a position of weakness. But that is not true. Respect and submission are not given from a place of weakness, but rather a position of strength—God's strength.

As I have mentioned before, each of us are to work out our own salvation in the reverent fear of God. That's what He says in Philippians 2:12. This means we are to *cooperate* with His Spirit's correction and direction, adjusting our lives to His will. But we don't do that in our own strength. The very next verse reveals this...

"[Not in your own strength] for it is God Who is all the while effectually at work in you [energizing and creating in you the power and desire], both to will and to work for His good pleasure *and* satisfaction *and* delight."

Did you catch that? *God* gives you the power and desire to do His will—it is *not* in your own strength! The ability to submit to and respect your husband comes from the position of God's energizing strength. Even if your husband has treated you terribly, God will create in you the power and desire to forgive him and move on.

Forgiving Allen was not easy, and I can honestly say I didn't really want to at first. After holding his head under water emotionally for a very long time, God lovingly called me on the carpet about my attitude. As I continued to read and study His Word, the Holy Spirit began to show me my unwillingness to share the same mercy and forgiveness that I myself had received. I was refusing to give mercy to the person who was supposed to be my nearest and dearest friend. This reality check melted my heart.

But why? Why did I withhold mercy and forgiveness? I didn't trust him—plain and simple. I had been hurt by him and others countless times, and I was afraid of being hurt again. Unknowingly, I withheld mercy and forgiveness in an attempt to protect myself from further pain. It didn't work.

TRUST IS KEY

In order to submit to your husband, letting go and allowing him to take control, you must be able to trust. Again, this is not something you can do in your own strength. The strength to trust comes from God. Over time and through experience, your trust will grow. It is a process.

Years ago I heard someone say, "Your relationship with your husband reflects your relationship with God." Initially, I refused to believe that. But not believing it didn't stop it from being true. If we don't trust our husbands, then there is a trust issue with God. If we won't respect our husbands, then there is a rebellion issue with God.

To be quite honest, there are still times I struggle with the issue of trust. To help me overcome this, I have placed sticky notes all over my house saying, "Trust each other's good will!" I got the idea from *Love and Respect*, Dr. Emerson Eggerichs' teachings on marriage. He and his wife, Sarah, remind us that, "None of us married someone that we thought hated us and did not want the best for us." This is so important to remember.

I can recall a time when I didn't question my man's "good will" toward me and even felt loved when he took charge. But like so many other women do, I lost sight of this truth somewhere along the way. I was hurt or thought I was being mistreated and held onto that hurt and all the others that followed. As a result, I developed an attitude of *I will not surrender!* I dug in my heels, got into a fighting stance and did everything I could to get my way. Life became miserable for us. Can you relate?

Thank God it doesn't have to stay that way. You and I can choose to forgive our men daily and receive God's grace (strength and power) to respect and submit to them in a healthy way. Without forgiveness and trust, it is impossible to honor them from our hearts as God wants.

We really can do all things, even the things we thought impossible, through Christ who gives us strength (see Philippians 4:13). Only with His strength can we respect and submit to our husbands from a place of strength and control.

God will gladly give us His power as we give Him control of our lives.

THE MANIPULATION STIPULATION

While we are being real and honest with ourselves, let's chat for a bit about manipulation. To *manipulate* means "to influence or manage shrewdly or deviously; to tamper with or falsify for personal gain."[2] Simply said, manipulation is the attempt to control others for our own good.

I think you will agree that we all have a little "Delilah" in us (see Judges 16:4-21). Can I get a witness? We all know how to manipulate our man and get what we want, when we want it. Though this is natural to us from birth, it is not God's will for our marriages. In fact, looking back at the times that I've manipulated Allen, I ended up regretting it every time in a **big** way!

It was a sad day when I came face to face with the fact that I was a manipulator. I just didn't see that about myself. How, I don't know. It is so obvious to me now that anyone who lives as I did, on the streets doing a lot of drugs and alcohol, has to be a major manipulator in some way. Of course, being a manipulator is not limited to those who have my background; *everyone* has the capability within them. Addicts just have more practice and are better at it.

Thankfully, God didn't show me I was a manipulator to overwhelm me, nor did He want me to take matters into my own hands and try to change myself. He showed me my heart so I would run to Him for help. He was after the root issue behind the behavior. Manipulation is the fruit of a deeper root—fear. For most, it is a survival tactic to stay in control of our lives and avoid more hurt.

I know...it doesn't make sense in our minds to give up caring for our needs. If we don't do it, who will, right? But continuing to try to control everything will wear us out. Trust me...I know. By the time I quit drinking all the "liquid courage" (alcohol) that I could find and God showed me I was a manipulator, I was exhausted. I was tired of trying to control everything and everybody—tired of constantly trying to get my way.

As I purposed more and more to be in God's will, I learned to trust Him little by little. The evidence that proved this trust came by allowing Him to sit in the front seat more often. The fruit of that kind of trust is peace. That's the faithfulness of God. His Word confirms this, declaring,

> **"You will keep in perfect peace all who *trust* in you, all whose thoughts are fixed on you!"**
>
> **—Isaiah 26:3 NLT**

One of the lies the devil uses to hold us hostage in fear is that if we respect and submit to our husbands *without* being manipulators, we will have to give up everything. We will end up becoming like a doormat to be walked on.

But this is not so, my sweet sisters! The only things God wants us to give up are those that keep us in bondage and separated from true freedom in Him. I have never felt more peace and freedom than when I rest in trusting our heavenly Father. The key is having our minds fixed and then fixing our minds on the right things.

LOVE CHOOSES TO LOOK BEYOND THE UGLY
TO SEE THE BEAUTIFUL

What we focus our minds on will either produce life or death in our marriages. In each of us, there is good, bad, and ugly. For far too long, I focused only on the bad and the ugly in Allen. If he did something wrong, I usually never forgot it, nor did I let him forget it. It seemed as if I wasn't capable of seeing any of the good things he did. Once again, I was in line to learn a lesson.

One of those lessons came while I was grilling up some bratwurst for dinner one evening. In between trips to the BBQ pit, I was reading a book by Bunny Wilson, *Liberated Through Submission: God's Design for Freedom in All Relationships!*—a book I highly recommend to better your marriage.

Suddenly, the Lord drew my attention to a row of trees along our fence line. These trees were dense and in desperate need of pruning. In fact, they were downright ugly. It was hard to see through them. They were old, gnarly, and packed with dead branches. In my heart, I knew there was something the Holy Spirit wanted me to see on the other side of them. After struggling for a while trying to see beyond the ugly, I was finally able to concentrate my focus and see some beautiful orange flowers blooming on the other side.

Within moments, it hit me. My view of Allen was like that of the trees. All I could see was his desperate need for spiritual pruning. On the surface, his old dead ways were staring me in the face. But there was something beautiful on the other side of all the ugly that the Holy Spirit wanted me to see.

God expanded this lesson a few years later when I underwent major surgery on my lower back. For several months, I was completely incapacitated. I wasn't even able to put on my own socks and shoes as I learned how to walk again. Although we were radically blessed by the help of our family and friends during that time, Allen was my main caretaker.

When I reached the point where I no longer needed a full-time babysitter, he went back to work. Each morning before he left, he made sure I was set up for the day with everything I needed. He would work all day, come home and do all the cooking and cleaning, and also shop for groceries. My loving man kicked some butt and took names as he stepped up to the challenge.

One day when I was finally able to get up and piddle around the house, I went and took a peek into our freshly stocked pantry. As I surveyed its contents, my eye caught sight of a brand we normally didn't use. Instantly, I became frustrated, mumbling and grumbling out loud to myself. Instead of being grateful for him doing what I couldn't do, I started to go into that ugly nagging and ragging mode. By God's grace, I caught myself in mid grumble and stopped.

I then did something I hadn't had the wherewithal to do for a long time. I started saying out loud, "Thank You, God, that I have a husband who goes grocery shopping! Thank You that he went to the store when I couldn't. Thank You! Thank You! Thank You, Lord!" As I did this, the angry, negative thoughts were replaced with thoughts of gratitude and praise. This was indeed a breakthrough.

Proverbs 18:21 (AMP) declares, "Death and life are in the power of the tongue...." This principle was clearly confirmed that day. Life was being generated in me as I voiced thanks. God was fixing me as I fixed my mind and mouth on the good in Allen instead of the bad and ugly. This is the timeless truth of Philippians 4:8-9:

"Summing it all up, friends, I'd say you'll do best by filling your minds and meditating on things true, noble, reputable, authentic, compelling, gracious—the best, not the worst; the beautiful, not the ugly; things to praise, not things to curse. Put into practice what you learned from me, what you heard and saw and realized. Do that, and God, who makes everything work together, will work you into his most excellent harmonies."

—The Message

God, who had begun a good work in my heart years earlier, was being faithful to His Word to continue that work (see Philippians 1:6). I have learned, the more I fellowship with the Lord in His Word, prayer and worship, the easier it becomes to successfully look past things that frustrate me. Time in His presence and obedience to His promptings is how the fruit of His Spirit grows in our lives. (Check out Galatians 5 for life-changing scriptures on freedom in Christ, living by the Spirit, the acts of the flesh and the fruit of the Spirit.)

I've had the privilege of sharing with you some sweet moments Allen and I have had over the years. I thank God for those times and for Him helping me to focus on them. We all need to be able to see and focus on the good. Yes, there will be bad and ugly that comes, but we don't have to camp there. With a willing heart and effort on our part, we can refocus on the good and the beautiful things in our men. As we make this worthy investment, we will enjoy a huge return!

THE MOMENT OF TRUTH

I opened this lesson with the story of Allen finding a lump on his neck, and that is where I will pick up and close. Indeed it was an adventurous time of testing—a moment of truth you might say. I am embarrassed and humbled to admit that in my selfishness, my attitude toward him did not really change markedly until he found that lump. His dire situation opened my eyes to see him in a whole new light.

After our trip to the mountains, we returned to the doctor as promised. The lump had not left. Surgery was scheduled, and it was promptly removed. After a biopsy, it was determined to be a cancerous lymph node. It was the same cancer my Grandfather died from. This procedure was followed by a more extensive surgery—the removal of a tumor from Allen's tongue and throat, along with a select neck dissection. In that portion of the surgery they removed over seventy lymph nodes, a saliva gland and other various tissues.

This was followed by the removal of the majority of his teeth in preparation for thirty-three treatments of radiation. I had never seen my husband so sick. The radiation depleted his body so badly he needed IV fluids and a suction machine to keep him from choking to death. A feeding tube was surgically inserted into his stomach for feedings and medications every two hours 24/7.

I am so grateful to be able to say that after losing ninety pounds and most of his strength, Allen did recover. He returned to work much sooner than anyone expected. This freaked out his primary doctor the first time he saw him. He had received a number of reports from both the surgeon and radiologist charting how sick Allen had been. He couldn't believe Allen was as healthy as he was and already working full time again. We praise God for His healing and grace through it all.

Now you would think I remained a good girl and lived happily ever after with my man after all that, right? Wrong. The truth is, while he was sick, there were a couple of times I got very stern with him. He had been such a good patient for a long time, and then one day he turned into a real jerk. God had helped me brush off his harshness several times and not take it personally. But when his 3:30 am feeding and medication time came and he gave me more of the same bad attitude, I let it fly.

I assertively, but gently said to him, "I am doing the best I can to take care of you and I don't deserve your harsh treatment. I love you. Because I love you, I am choosing to take care of you. But I can bail on you at any time. And if that's what you want, then by all means continue to treat me like crap."

Believe it or not, God really helped me tame my tongue. I didn't talk to him in a mean, nagging way, and because of this, he saw my heart and stopped that behavior. Out of this lengthy life or death mess, God produced many miracles and this was one of them.

Isn't It Time to Tighten *Your* Faucet?

After twenty-six years of marriage, the aim of my heart is to not be a drip on the rest of my husband's trip. I want to respect him and submit willingly to his leadership, and I encourage you to do the same. Again, God's Word says,

"In the same way, you wives must accept the authority of your husbands. Then, even if some refuse to obey the Good News, your godly lives will speak to them without any words. They will be won over by observing your pure and reverent lives. Don't be concerned about the outward beauty of fancy hairstyles, expensive jewelry, or beautiful clothes."

—1 Peter 3:1-3 NLT

I want to make it clear that submission and respect do not mean we become our husband's punching bag, physically or verbally. There are times it is appropriate to be assertive and draw some boundaries for ourselves. But give God a chance to defend you first, give you favor, and meet your needs. What will make the difference is your heart attitude.

Yes, I know our men have made mistakes, said things in anger, and not loved us the way we needed at times. But if we truly want to be wives who do only good to our husbands and not harm as Proverbs 31:12 describes, then we must consider God's wisdom in what our husbands need from us—respect and submission.

Right now you may be frustrated with the relationship between you and your husband. Maybe you have slipped back into a pattern of being a nagging, ragging drip. If so, it's time to tighten your faucet and get a grip on your lip. Check the oil level of the Holy Spirit in you. Maybe you need a spiritual tune-up from the Master Mechanic. If so, just ask. He's on duty 24/7.

Don't wait until you almost lose your husband to treat him better like I did. Repent of your attitude toward him and allow God to turn your frustration into a new level of trust in Him. Surrender yourself and your marriage to His care, and in time He will turn it around.

Lesson Summary

Something to Hold On To

As women, we all have the capability to nag, rag and manipulate our husbands. But that's not what they need or what God wants us to give them. Our men need respect and submission. Maybe you're like me and have a lot of pain from your past. God will give you His grace to work through it as you surrender yourself to Him. Even if your husband has treated you terribly, God will create in you the power and desire to forgive him and give him respect. Yes, it is a tall order, but with God all things are possible! Not only am I living proof, but there are countless others who prove God's Word and His promises to be true.

Rena's playlist:

- "You Are for Me" ~ by Kari Jobe

- "Resting" ~ live version by Rita Springer

- "In the Palm of Your Hand" ~ by Alison Kraus and The Cox Family

Questions for personal or group reflection:

- What does a picture of genuine respect and submission look like to you? Do you give this to your husband? If so, how do you do it? If not, why?

- Where does the ability to respect, trust, and submit to your husband come from? How do you receive it? What practical things can you do to show greater respect and submission?

- Look at your relationship with your spouse and with God. In what ways do they reflect one another? Is the Holy Spirit prompting you to make any changes? If so, what are they?

- Carefully meditate on Philippians 4:8. Write a list of positive things about your husband that you can begin fixing your mind and mouth on. Do this once a day for 30 days and journal what happens.

- What is your greatest "take away" from this lesson—
  what came alive and jumped off the pages that you
  want to remember?

---

[1]"The Power of Respect Talk," By Dr. Emerson Eggerichs (http://
loveandrespect.com/blog/power-of-respect-talk, retrieved 6/15/12).
[2] Definition of *Manipulate* (http://www.thefreedictionary.com/
manipulate, retrieved 6/14/12)

"When we face an impossible situation, all self-reliance and self-confidence must melt away; we must be totally dependent on Him for the resources."

—Anne Graham Lotz[1]

Lesson 5

Wow!
He *Finally* Got *It!*

For nothing is impossible with God.

Luke 1:37 NLT

We were on the road again, heading to Virginia this time! My man and I were on a mission to buy a salvaged 2000 Heritage Springer Softail. We may not have been on a bike, but we were going to get one, which was almost as good.

As men often do, mine wanted to conquer this trip and claim his prize. He was thrilled about the deal he had found. He had come across a slightly wrecked, but prayerfully fixable, piece of "man toy," and the price was right!

Upon beginning our adventure, Allen laid out the ground rules so I would know what to expect. Wasn't that sweet of him? He said, "We're gonna drive straight thru to Virginia and make the deal or not, depending on the condition of the bike. After that, we can do whatever you want. We'll even get a hotel room for the night *and* get you a rock from every state. Whatcha think?"

I have to tell you, right then and there my heart swelled with that wonderful warm feeling of gushy love toward my husband. I was thrilled and eagerly agreed to his plan.

The Journey Begins

As we made our way to Virginia, we had a blast and actually enjoyed each other's company. We reached our destination in good time and in good spirits. When we arrived at the sales lot, Allen didn't waste any time; he immediately began checking out the bike. After a good once over, he knew it would take some effort, skill and grace from God to fix the wrecked front end. But he decided to go for it. He made his offer, and the deal was done.

Surprisingly to both of us, I trusted his judgment. This was one of the first times I remember fully trusting a decision of his while I was sober. It felt so good to be able to allow myself to relax in his leadership.

With the new bike strapped in the bed of our truck, we began cruising the scenic route through Virginia's Blue Ridge Mountains.

Wow! He Finally Got It!

I was bursting at the seams with excitement to see God's awe-inspiring scenery. Such beauty He has created!

Allen was very pleased with the way things had gone with the bike deal as well as with me. In my totally rapturous state and agreeable spirit, he couldn't help but pour out his love on me. He did this by offering to let me hop in the back of the truck and sit on the bike as we finished driving through the scenic highway. He wanted me to finally be able to say I had ridden through the mountains on a bike, something neither of us had done yet.

Again, my heart warmed as I was overwhelmed with the realization that he was *finally* getting *it*. It was such a sweet offer full of his love toward me. I kindly declined his loving proposition and decided instead to scoot real close to him and lay a big smooch on his cheek. There I remained, next to my man, clinging tightly to him as we enjoyed the view together.

The rest of the trip was just as amazing as the beginning. We stayed at a hotel for the night and began making our way home the next morning. We traveled through West Virginia, Ohio, Indiana, and Illinois all the way to our home in Missouri.

As Allen promised, we picked up a rock in every state...until we got to Illinois. The rock-free fields we passed through were quite a disappointment. For several hours we searched and searched and had almost given up hope. Finally, just before crossing the border into Missouri, we snagged a *little* gem for exportation. Mission complete!

We accomplished everything my man had said we would. I was very impressed with his dedication to keep his word. After spending several extra hours hunting for that final rock, it was obvious he was really trying to give me what he knew I wanted.

This definitely earned him extra bonus points! As a sweet friend once told me, "When you have a man that is trying, you've got a lot!" And boy was she right.

HE REALLY WAS *FINALLY* GETTING *IT*!

What is "it," you ask? "It" is that I am just GOO-GOO over rocks. As I mentioned in Lesson 1, I love 'em! I can't get enough of 'em! I want some more of 'em! Now, I know that may sound weird coming from a chick, but I tend to lean toward weird. So much so that Allen has declared, "One day I will write my own book, *Life with the Weird Chick.*"

What it took for Allen to get *it* was for him to see my friend's husband bring me back a rock from Colorado a few weeks before we left on our trip to buy the bike. This was not just an ordinary rock either, it was an *awesome* rock.

Di and "Daddy" Bruce, as we call him, go to Colorado every year to ride four-wheelers and dirt bikes in the mountains. When they go, they always bring back lots of rocks, and I just go goo-goo over them.

After returning from their last trip, they invited us over to visit and look at pictures. As we were leaving, we walked outside among all the rocks lying in their driveway. Yep, you guessed it; I was drooling and coveting those big, beautiful rocks.

Now you have to know our friend Daddy Bruce. He's a funny guy. While we were outside admiring his new "little babies," he began asking me which ones I liked the most.

"So, Rena," he said, as he pointed to one rock and then another, "How ya like that one?"

Again and again, he asked me the same question, all the way up to the last rock. With this one, however, his goofy ear to ear grin really shined though his Fu-man-Chu mustache. "And what about this one right here?"

"Well...it's great," I replied. "But it's not as cool as that one!" as I pointed to one we had already gone over. Suddenly, the grin left his face. He began to share how he had handpicked the last rock he pointed to especially for me.

I was blown away. I couldn't believe he had taken time while on *his* vacation to pick out a rock just for me. Wow! Much to my delight and rock *goo-goo-ness*, he gave me my favorite pick and loaded it into the back of our truck. Not only was I blessed with a beautiful rock, I was also blessed by a lesson in love that my man observed.

You Really *Can* Teach an Old Dog New Tricks... and Even Learn a Few Yourself!

Sometimes we all need a little help figuring out the things of life—even the simplest ones. This includes learning how to love our husbands (and wives). I don't know why it works this way, but it seems to be universally true. When we are young, we are generally naïve with thoughts of love's grandeur. We are "absolutely sure" that our marriage will never have to be worked on and we will remain in wedded bliss forever. Then reality hits. We grow older and as time passes we become tired of trying and failing to speak our spouse's love language. The truth is, we need to be taught that our marriages need regular maintenance, and that maintenance requires effort. You should never quit trying.

Throughout our previous years together, Allen had sporadically tried to do things to show me his love and make me happy. Since he didn't know exactly what that looked like, his efforts lessened as time went by. Some of this was my fault because I, myself, didn't know what made me happy. When I thought I had finally figured out what *it* was, *it* would change. This gave Allen a moving target to shoot at. It's no wonder it was difficult for him to hit it. He was actually set up to fail and neither of us even knew it.

When we started going to church, we received help to live a different way than we had been living. One helpful thing we learned on the subject of relationships is that what says "I love you" to one, may not say "I love you" to the other.

Dr. Gary Chapman has served as a marriage counselor for over thirty years. In his bestselling book, *The Five Love Languages*, he identifies five basic ways we receive and give love. They are: Words of Affirmation, Quality Time, Receiving Gifts, Acts of Service, and Physical Touch.

Dr. Chapman shares that the reason we often fail to speak each other's "love language" is because we tend to love others in the way *we* want to be loved. If we want to succeed in our efforts to express love, we must consider what really says "I love you" to the other person, even if it is different than what says "I love you" to us.

That day at Di and Bruce's house seven years ago, my man observed how excited I was over something as simple as a rock. He learned what says, "I love you" to me. As a wise student does with the things he learns, Allen tucked that little factoid away to be used at an opportune time. And use it is just what he did.

The best way to really learn something is to put it into practice, reinforcing the information. Actually doing *it* causes *it* to become more than just head knowledge. My husband has always been a very smart man, but in recent years he has kicked it up a notch and become a wise man. This was proven on our sweet trip to the mountains when he pulled out and put into practice quite a few concepts I didn't even know he had learned.

One of those concepts was from a marriage Sunday school class we had attended thirteen years earlier. It was from a study we did by seasoned marriage author and speaker, Gary Smalley. One of the things he taught is that vacations and trips should have something in them that is a "Ten" for everyone in the family. We had not practiced that principle much after we had heard it, but our trip to Virginia had that lesson all over it!

What was Allen's idea of a "Ten" on that trip? It was driving and conquering the miles, negotiating the sale, and then going in for the kill...I mean, buying his toy. The playing out of this scenario made my man a happy biker as we left the dealer that day. And I must say, there was something really sexy about all that testosterone-driven manliness!

My idea of a "Ten" was slowing down and enjoying the awesome scenery. This, of course, included looking at and gathering **rocks**, along with finding a nice hotel for the night. That made me one happy camper—hotel camper, that is.

This trip marked a new season in our marriage of learning how to say "I love you" in ways that the other one could hear it. Allen started bringing me rocks that he found for no special reason. My favorite Valentine's Day gift over the years is when my man, the student of love that he now is, gave me a homemade card, a single rose and a beautiful new rock. This made a huge deposit in my love bank. Cha-ching!

THE REAL DEAL

I've got a feeling some of you are doing that little gesture thingy right now. You know, the one where you act like you are about to make yourself puke with your fingers in your throat. I can see ya. Really, I can. I can see y'all doing that because I have done the same thing more than once and probably not too long ago—especially early on in my Christian walk.

Anytime I heard someone share something that oozed sweetness, I would just about gag. I didn't know anyone who acted that way before we started going to church. So when I met someone who did, I was rather skeptical and questioned their sincerity. Sometimes I was right and their actions proved to be too good to be true. But every now and then the person turned out to be "the real deal." They had done the work it took to get *it* for their husband or wife and it showed. God was glorified in their **real and imperfect,** yet *sweet* relationship.

The more Allen and I saw *real* love in action in other marriages, the more we longed for it in our own. We knew before we were married that something was missing and very wrong, but we just kept doing the things we knew to do. Sadly, nothing ever changed. But when we started learning the truth of what God wants for His children, we began to have hope. For the first time, we began to believe our relationship could get better. And maybe, just maybe, with God's help, our marriage would someday glorify Him.

Please keep in mind that our trip to Virginia was in 2005. Allen and I first met in 1981 when I was fifteen. We began dating off and on when I was sixteen and started living together when I was nineteen. In 1986 I turned twenty-one, and we got married. Our trip to Virginia was twenty-four years after we had met, nineteen

116

years after we were married, and fourteen years after we accepted Jesus as our Lord and Savior and began living for Him to the best of our ability.

This trip was a marked time when we *finally* began seeing glimpses of us becoming "the real deal." So I think you can give us just a moment to ooze a little sweetness. Haven't we *finally* earned it?

THE PAINFUL POSITION OF TRANSITION

This hassle-free trip was a long time coming. Not that we didn't have some good moments over the previous years. We actually had quite a few, but that's all they were—*moments*. Sure, we liked each other some of the time. That is, until a little stress crept in or one of us didn't like what the other had said. There was a multitude of minor irritants that always seemed to blow up into a major ordeal.

In a lot of ways, things actually got worse before they got better. Once we invited Jesus into our lives, we did a complete 180-degree turn from many of our old ways. Yes, life was new and fresh and God had softened our hearts. But in the area of our marriage, we kept going back to our old preprogrammed ways. We tried hard not to, but while we were relearning to deal with daily issues in a healthy way, we had a lot of fights. You could say, "We got it on like Donkey Kong!" During the painful time of transition, we were ready to quit almost daily.

My weapon of choice to control situations was throwing the "d" bomb out in heated arguments. While the threat of *divorce* was effective, it was also very hurtful. In my mind, I was convinced Allen would one day leave me like everyone else in my life had. My way of dealing with this fear was to always give him (and everyone else who wanted to be a part of my life) a way out. It has just been in the last few years that I *really know* and trust that Allen is committed to me and our marriage. I didn't believe anyone could really know me and still love me—especially for as long as he has. But thank God he does.

As I have shared in the previous lessons, my life before Christ was nothing but extreme dysfunction and chaos. Because of this trauma, I thought I was damaged and broken beyond repair. God had to bring me back to the basics and teach me how to be a real person. This meant no more lying, hiding, running, or stuffing and covering up my feelings to keep me from blowing up. This was one of the reasons I got involved in a Christian twelve-step program at our church. As part of the program, I needed to make "a searching and *fearless* moral inventory of myself," which is the fourth step. Personally, the "fearless" part was a joke.

By the time I was done writing, I had pages and pages filled with all of my character defects—they were single spaced, both front and back. These were the things I needed to let go, but I was afraid to. I thought that if I let them go, there would be nothing left of me. Yet, I wholeheartedly wanted to be empty of everything that was not of God, and it couldn't happen fast enough. So I pressed on. I later learned in a sermon from our pastor, "The Blessing of Being Empty," that being empty is a good thing. God can't fill us with Himself until we're empty of ourselves.

Emptying ourselves of *us* is another way of saying crucifying our flesh. John the Baptist said it this way: "I must decrease so that He (Jesus) can increase" (see John 3:30). This is all a part of working out your salvation. Just as we learned in Lesson 4, you must remember that the way to do this is "[Not in your own strength] for it is **God Who is all the while effectually at work**

in you [energizing and creating in you the power and desire], both to will and to work for His good pleasure *and* satisfaction *and* delight" (Philippians 2:13 AMP).

Just like the bratty boy, Eustace, in C.S. Lewis' classic story, *The Voyage of the Dawn Treader*, we cannot remove our scaly, dragon-like skin in our own strength. God has to do it. All that He requires us to do is to willingly cooperate with His Spirit and not fight against Him.

When I *finally* allowed the Holy Spirit to begin the process of peeling off the layers of junk that had built up over the course of my life, the healing began. Oh, He had to go deep into my core. It hurt so bad at times that I thought I would literally die. But I was desperate for change. Amazingly, I was on the right track to experiencing God's better way of living.

Meanwhile, Allen was going through his own process of transformation. God was doing a huge work in him as well. The sad thing was it still wasn't showing up in our marriage. Our hearts had changed in many ways, but our actions and reactions to each other had not caught up yet. We kept doing what we had always done, butchering each other with our words. We left each other for dead more times than we can count. We knew we had to do something different and *finally* decided to act on it.

ARE YOU *FINALLY* GONNA DO SOMETHING OR JUST STAND THERE AND BLEED?

Knowing we needed to do something different to get different results, we attempted to apply a tourniquet to our marriage in the form of prayer and seeking wise counsel from someone we trusted. We learned that the two generations of divorce in my family had to be dealt with spiritually so that it would not be repeated in our marriage and then passed down to our daughters.

Encouraged by friends and nudged by the Holy Spirit, we decided to act on our new knowledge by going to the altar for prayer one Sunday evening at church. At first we were tempted to harden our hearts in pride and stay in our seats, but God's grace was there empowering us to step out in obedience. By divine appointment our pastor, Ed Shirrell who came from a family of divorce himself, was there to pray for us. God always knows and provides the best person for the job!

We laid it all out and held nothing back. We confessed the generational sin of divorce in my family and our constant fighting, according to the instructions in James 5:16. Putting on a plastic smile and pretending like everything was okay was out of the question. We were bleeding to death internally and desperately needed and wanted to be healed. Our honesty and humility with God, ourselves and others set the stage for healing to begin.

Pastor Shirrell was a powerful prayer warrior for us that night. As he began to pray, he was led to walk around us seven times, just as God had told Joshua to do when Israel went up against the city of Jericho (see Joshua 2). Once again, He faithfully came through. Just as the walls of Jericho fell, the walls of division, strife and bitterness that had been built up in our marriage began to crumble. From that day on, I stopped using the threat of divorce as a weapon, both offensively and defensively. Yes, I've had a few slips over the years, but they are nothing in comparison to the way I used to act. God began a deep work that day. Although the hemorrhaging had stopped, there was still a lot of hard work to be done.

Wow! He Finally Got It!

TRANSFORMED FROM BEING INCAPACITATED TO FACILITATORS OF HEALING

One of the places both Allen and I received healing and learned how to love was through a *Love and Respect Marriage Conference* we attended in 2007. These special teaching sessions were given by Dr. Emerson Eggerichs and his wife, Sarah. In them they describe the major differences between men and women. Dr. Emerson offers a clever comparison, saying that the way men see, hear, and speak is like looking at life through "blue sunglasses." On the other hand, women see, hear, and speak through the shade of "pink." For men, they communicate and relate through the "blue" lens of *respect*. For women, it's the "pink" spectacles of *love*. Neither one is wrong. They are just different, and understanding this difference is the key to healing and harmony within marriage.

Dr. Emerson and his wife strongly convey how God designed men, and they don't make them feel like dogs for being that way. Allen thought this was one of the best marriage resources he had ever seen or heard. He liked it so much he bought the DVDs and a case of workbooks with the intention of starting a small group. Five years later, we are doing it!

God has transformed us from being incapacitated to facilitators of healing. No, our marriage is not perfect and never will be. But we have grown to the point of *finally* being able to help others. We are working with two couples who are dear friends that have similar issues as us. With the train load of baggage between us all, we felt we could trust each other. This has allowed us to be real and support one another through some tough issues. I want to encourage you to find a group such as this one, where you can be real so you can heal.

As facilitators, we have poured a lot of prayer into our small group. We know that if we aren't willing to work at doing what we are teaching, it will hurt God and be a terrible waste of everyone's time. You can't help others do what you're not willing to try to do yourself.

During this time of prayer, the Lord has shown me that those of us who have had such "colorful" backgrounds before coming to Christ are striving to get to some normalcy in our lives. In other words, we are trying to move from viewing life through the lenses of *black* and *red* to viewing it through *blue* and *pink*. No easy task even with God's help, especially when those coming from the cute blue and pink have enough struggles of their own.

What does *black* and *red* look like? When Allen and I first met, we were drunk. When we got married and for the five years that followed we were still drunk. When we sobered up, we didn't have a clue who we were as individuals nor did we know who we were as a couple.

Ultimately, the goal of each couple is oneness—both seeing life through the same lens of purple. So if things don't change overnight, don't be surprised or discouraged. Yes, those of us *black* and *red* folks have to work harder sometimes. But God's grace is there for all of us to *finally* do something about *it*!

BABY, YOU'VE COME TOO FAR TO GIVE UP NOW!

Chapter 5 of the Gospel of Mark tells of a series of miraculous healings at the hands of Jesus. First, He delivered a man possessed with a legion of demons. Immediately afterward, a grieved father named Jairus asked Jesus to come and heal his little girl who was deathly sick. As He began to make His way to her, a woman who had been bleeding for twelve years was healed when she reached out and touched the hem of His robe. Her faith in Christ had made her whole.

At that point, friends of Jairus arrived to tell him that his daughter had died. Since the situation seemed hopeless, they didn't see any point in bothering Jesus any longer. Even after seeing and hearing of the miraculous things Jesus had just done, they doubted His ability. God, who knows all things, knew the father of the little girl had given up, but He was not finished yet. The Scripture says,

"Overhearing what they said, Jesus told him, 'Don't be afraid; just believe.'"

—Mark 5:36 NIV

Jesus then went to the man's home, approached his daughter's bedside and said, "Little girl, arise," Instantly, the little girl awoke. She was raised from the dead by Christ, the Resurrection and the Life!

In the same way, my sweet sisters, Jesus is saying to you "Don't be afraid; just believe!" Although your marriage seems dead, don't give up hope. He wants you to stick with it for just a little while longer and believe that with Him *all things are possible.* Stop now and listen to the quiet whisper of your Savior. It's just what you need to push past the temptation to quit. You've come too far to give up now!

YOUR MARRIAGE IS WORTH FIGHTING FOR!

The society we live in today has made relationships and even life itself cheap and disposable. Many have forgotten what it really means to commit to something and fight for it. But marriages are not disposable as many would like us to believe. I am eternally grateful to God for opening our eyes to the fact that our marriage is worth fighting for! Yours is too! But you have to push past the easy outs, the cute one-liner clichés and all the quick, Band-Aid remedies. Allen and I tried all those, and they're useless. To finally get *it* will take time, effort and patience.

Again, what is *it,* you ask? Well, if you haven't figured it out, *it* really isn't about rocks, nor is *it* about the fluff of the material things that won't matter in the end. *It* is simply caring about the things that are really important—first to our heavenly Father and then to each other. *It* is the things worth fighting for, such as being true to your word and honoring your commitments. *It* is doing what is right, even when *it* is kicking you in the butt because *it* is so dog-gone hard. Lastly, *it* is choosing to ignore everyone who is telling you to take the easy way out and instead pressing in to trust God for transformation and new life.

IT IS REAL **LOVE!**

What does real love look like? God gives us an awesome picture:

"Love is patient and kind. Love is not jealous or boastful or proud or rude. *It* does not demand its own way. *It* is not irritable, and *It* keeps no record of being wronged. *It* does not rejoice about injustice but rejoices whenever the truth wins out. Love never gives up, never loses faith, is always hopeful, and endures through every circumstance."

—1 Corinthians 13:4-7 NLT

If no one has ever told you, let me be the first to say it. Your marriage is worth fighting for. *It is so worth It!* If you have struggled as Allen and I have, I know you are dog tired and have felt so alone at times. But hold on and don't lose heart or lose grip of the One who is holding you. He will see you through. I promise! Better yet, God promises! He says,

> **"And let us not lose heart and grow weary and faint in acting nobly and doing right, for in due time and at the appointed season we shall reap, if we do not loosen and relax our courage and faint."**

> **—Galatians 6:9 AMP**

As the title of this lesson states, my man *finally* got *it*. But if we hadn't gotten help from God and other believers in the Church, we would have never gotten that chance. If just one of us had quit during one of those hundreds of times we wanted to, I would not have the confidence to share with you that no matter how hard it gets, the work is worth *it*! God's grace and love will see you through even the hardest of days so that you and your man will one day *finally* get *it* too!

Lesson Summary

<u>Something to Hold On To</u>

Just like the wrecked bike we rescued from the salvage yard, God rescued us and our marriage. He is in the salvage business. It took a lot of effort to restore the bike, and our wrecked marriage has required no less. As we continue to strive for God's best in our marriages and do our part, **we will finally get it!**

Though you and your husband may now see life through black and red lenses, you have the potential to one day come together and see life through the same colored lenses of vibrant purple, becoming a beautiful work of LOVE that glorifies our heavenly Father!

"May you experience the love of Christ, though it is too great to understand fully. Then you will be made complete with all the fullness of life and power that comes from God. Now all glory to God, who is able, through his mighty power at work within us, to accomplish infinitely more than we might ask or think" (Ephesians 3:19-20 NLT).

Rena's playlist:

- "God Gave Me You (for the Ups and Downs)" ~ by Dave Barnes

- "You're Not Alone" ~ by Meredith Andrews

- "Take Heart" ~ by Hillsong

Questions for personal or group reflection:

- What's your man's love language? What says, "I love you" to him and really makes him light up with joy and gratitude? If you don't know, study him to find out. Take the Love Language quiz at http://www.5lovelanguages.com/assessments/30-second-quizzes/love/.

- Why is it so important to be empty of yourself? How is this done—what is your part in the process and God's part? (Check out Philippians 2:12-13 for help.)

- Honesty and humility with God, yourself, and others is what sets the stage for healing to begin. Have you been honest and humble with God, yourself, and your spouse? Take time to do so now.

- Are you ready to quit on your marriage? Do you feel you've tried everything and nothing is working? Get quiet before God and ask Him what to do. Write what He reveals and do it.

- What is your greatest "take away" from this lesson—what came alive and jumped off the pages that you want to remember?

---

[1] *Fast Break, Five-Minute Devotions to Start Your Day* (Parable, 2007) Day 66.

"The beloved of God is no longer to sit in her past mistakes, abuses, and failures. A throne has been prepared for her. A position of delegated authority awaits her. She is to rest in this position, exercising and enjoying the rights and privileges it provides. This throne is for God's children...."

—Lisa Bevere[1]

Lesson 6

Unnecessary
Burdens

Praise the Lord, who carries our burdens day after day;
he is the God who saves us.

Psalm 68:19 GNT

Another major lesson I learned on our memorable road trip to Colorado was the lesson of *unnecessary burdens*. God taught me the importance of reevaluating our load and only holding on to what is needed—especially when plans change. Too much stuff makes the journey a drag.

As you may recall, Allen and I had planned on trailering our bike from St. Louis to North Platte, Nebraska. There we would connect with one of our good friends dropping the truck and trailer then riding to the mountains for a few days of play. Unfortunately, the truck broke down four hours from our friend Keith's home. Allen quickly determined that we had lost fifth gear and would not be able to continue the trip in that condition. Immediately, we started praying for direction on what to do.

We quickly exited the main highway and turned onto a rural road. It was about 6 p.m. on a weekday. There was a small car sales lot on one side of the highway and an even smaller trucking company on the other. We drove around both establishments, but there was no sign of life. It was as if we had entered the Twilight Zone. (insert strange music here)

As we began to pull out of the trucking company's parking lot, Allen paused and began gazing down the lonely country road in the opposite direction of the highway. In the far distance he saw a single plume of smoke rising into the dusky sky. Within an instant, he turned the rig around and began heading in the direction of the smoke signal.

After driving about a half mile, we saw that the smoke was rising from the direction of a small, one lane dirt road. As we turned onto the road, we soon realized it was a driveway that opened to reveal the cutest little farm nestled behind the trees. There was an eighteen-wheeler parked half inside and half outside of a huge garage. To the side of the massive doorway were two burn barrels with smoke pouring profusely from them.

Allen parked and got out. He found the owner of the farm under the eighteen-wheeler and up to his elbows in grease. I stayed in the truck praying and watching him explain our dilemma. The young man handed him a phone. Allen walked promptly to the side of the garage where it was quieter to talk. Moments later he returned, handed the phone back while shaking the farmer's hand. He jumped back into the truck and put it in gear.

"We're all set!" Allen said before I could even ask. "We're gonna drop the truck and trailer here and head out."

Now, I had been trying hard to be a "good wife" and not ask so many questions, but I still had a lot of growing to do. I like to be in the know most of the time. It seems to help me handle the times I don't get to know, if you know what I mean.

As you can imagine, the questions started flying. In one slick move, Allen gently and skillfully reached over and managed to squeeze my lips together between the rapid-fire of my questions. With my mouth closed, he filled me in on the rest of the details.

The person he spoke with on the phone was a good friend of the farm owner who just happened to own a transmission shop. How cool is that? He and Allen made all the necessary arrangements. The truck would be left at the farm; the transmission man would pick it up, take it to his shop, fix it, and return it before we returned in five days. All of this for the incredibly low price of $300. Allen had already told me that it would take no less than $1,200 to have it fixed back home.

Wow! God really came through! Although Allen was no longer holding my lips shut, miraculously I was still unable to utter a word. Just minutes earlier we were praying for help, and now I couldn't catch my breath for the help that had come so quickly. God is so good!

GOD'S PROVISION
SOMETIMES DEMANDS A DECISION

At the direction of the farm owner, we parked the truck and trailer off to the side. Our plan to save our bodies from having to ride the extra mileage on the bike had changed. It was now time to make some decisions about what we were going to take with us and what we were going to leave behind. Thus, we began the process of unpacking and repacking our "beast of burden."

The bike was originally packed with only the gear needed for the second leg of our trip. The trailer was packed with the things we needed for staying at our friend's house before we headed to Colorado. With this change of plans, we needed to repack our tour pack and saddle bags with **only the things necessary** for survival on the "whole trip" ahead.

With the bike finally reloaded and our leathers on, Allen handed the keys to the farmer and we peeled out for North Platte. The bike quickly found her "sweet spot" as Allen cracked open the throttle. Listening to the hum of the tires on the highway and the roar of our very loud pipes, I thought to myself, *What just happened? Are we completely crazy to surrender the truck so quickly to someone we don't even know?*

If you think about it, there were several decisions we had to make as God's provision became available. We had to decide to let go of our old plan so that we could grab the new plan. We also had to decide if we would trust the person God was using to provide for us. Though we didn't know him personally, we did know God. His Word says,

> **"Trust in the LORD with all your heart; do not depend on your own understanding. Seek his will in all you do, and he will show you which path to take."**
>
> **—Proverbs 3:5-6 NLT**

What an opportunity for Him to build our trust in Him. And that's exactly what He did.

NO WORRIES

After our awesome play date in the mountains came to an end, we retrieved the truck and loaded the bike back onto the trailer. We never did meet the man who did the work, but all was done as promised, except for one thing—the price for the repairs was different. Instead of charging us $300, he only charged us $250. Overwhelmed with gratefulness, we did the only thing a person should do in a situation such as ours. We gave the young farmer and his family the other $50.

Every time God does something amazing like this I end up asking myself, *Why do I worry?* Worry is an unnecessary burden we were never meant to carry. I don't know about you, but sometimes I get quite stressed trying to figure out how to meet all of my needs.

But God does not want us to worry about anything—period. Jesus makes this incredibly clear in Matthew 6:24-34. In verses 30-33, He says,

"If God gives such attention to the appearance of wildflowers—most of which are never even seen—don't you think he'll attend to you, take pride in you, do his best for you? What I'm trying to do here is to get you to relax, to not be so pre-occupied with *getting,* so you can respond to God's *giving.* People who don't know God and the way he works fuss over these things, but you know both God and how he works. Steep your life in God-reality, God-initiative, God-provisions. Don't worry about missing out. You'll find all your everyday human concerns will be met."

—Matthew 6:30-33 The Message

Why do we worry when God promises to take care of us? I believe one of the reasons is that we begin feeling like we don't deserve such love and attention. The truth is we don't. Did Allen and I deserve God's awesome display of provision and care? Nope...not a chance!

Think about all that He divinely arranged. Had our truck broken down any earlier, we would have probably found someone else to fix it. We would have paid a whole lot more and never met the young farm couple. And had we broken down any later, it would have been too dark to see the plume of smoke God used to guide us to our help. Interestingly, when we picked up the truck and began to share the workings of God's blessings, the farmer told us that he had never burned oil filters like he did that day—it was the first time.

It quickly became obvious that this was a God-thing—His fingerprints were all over it. There was not one thing we could have done ourselves to cause these things to happen. The only thing we did do was commit our trip to the Lord from the initial planning stages. We prayed and trusted Him for what we needed. He took care of the rest. Because of His faithful provision, we were able to fully enjoy the rest of our trip.

Again, God says,

> **"Therefore do not worry about tomorrow, for tomorrow will worry about itself. Each day has enough trouble of its own."**
>
> **—Matthew 6:34 NIV1984**

God's provision does not depend on us one bit! It is the unchanging goodness of His character that makes Him Jehovah Jireh, our Provider. He promises to provide for all our needs—spiritual, physical, financial, relational, vocational and emotional. And it's all according to His riches, not ours (see Philippians 4:19).

So don't spend your time and energy fretting over how your needs are going to get met. "Don't worry about anything; instead, pray about everything. Tell God what you need, and thank him for all he has done. Then you will experience God's peace, which exceeds anything we can understand. His peace will guard your hearts and minds as you live in Christ Jesus" (Philippians 4:6-7 NLT).

A Dog of an Object Lesson

When our girls were little, their grandpa gave them a sheltie puppy which we named Rocky. As he got older, we noticed a lump on his side. His long, thick fur hid it well, and it was only noticeable when we petted him. Over the years the lump grew, and our cute puppy began to look lopsided. It became apparent that one side of his body was much larger and disproportionate to the other, even under the camouflage of his fur.

We had our veterinarian take a look at Rocky. After the examination, she explained to us that it was just a fatty tumor and as long as it didn't affect any other organs, he would be fine. The surgery to remove the tumor would be costly—close to $300. And there was a possibility of it coming back if they didn't get all of it out. The good news was that he could carry it as long as he lived. He would just look strange.

A few years passed and it became obvious that Rocky's age was catching up with him. As a result of the growing tumor, he began to have trouble walking straight. The burden on his side was causing his balance to be uneven. Still, he loved to hang out with the family. One day while we were all outside cleaning up some brush along the side of the road, Rocky got caught underneath our trailer while Allen was moving it. He didn't get out of the way fast enough as he had in the past, and he got rolled.

We doctored him the best we could, making sure there were no broken bones or anything that required a vet's attention. Slowly but surely he recovered. As he did, we noticed that the extra weight of the tumor had become more of a burden to him than ever before.

Watching Rocky try to maneuver through daily life broke our hearts. One day as I observed him hobble across the room, I felt God speak two words to my heart, "unnecessary burdens." I then knew we had to do something.

But I'm a stay-at-home mom, I thought. *We only have one income and two teenage daughters still at home. How in the world can we afford it?* So, I began to pray for God to provide the money we needed to help our doggie. Within a week we received a statement from a transaction stating that we had overpaid a bill, and the company would be sending us a refund. It was just the amount we needed to pay for Rocky's surgery. God's provision is always right on time and He never asks us to do something without providing for it!

Believe it or not, the tumor weighed five pounds. Thankfully, it had not entwined itself with Rocky's ribs or affected any internal organs. As he healed from the surgery and was able to walk around, we noticed that he was still walking funny. It wasn't from the surgery; he actually was unable to compensate for the loss of the extra weight. Out of habit he walked as if he still had the tumor. It took him a while to relearn how to walk free from his burden, but he finally figured it out.

"MAY I HELP YOU WITH YOUR LUGGAGE?"

When God spoke the words *unnecessary burdens* to me, He wasn't just telling me about Rocky's tumor. I knew there was a profound lesson coming my way. He showed me that there are some things in life we were never meant to carry. These include fear, guilt, shame, worry, insecurity, hurts, bad habits, anger, rage, unforgiveness, bitterness, and every sin Jesus died to free us from.

There is a powerful verse in Hebrews that really nails this principle:

> **"Therefore then, since we are surrounded by so great a cloud of witnesses...let us strip off and throw aside every encumbrance (*unnecessary weight*) and that *sin* which so readily (deftly and cleverly) clings to and entangles us, and let us run with patient endurance and steady and active persistence the appointed course of the race that is set before us."**
>
> **—Hebrews 12:1 AMP**

When I first began walking with Jesus, my Savior and Friend, I was carrying a massive amount of unnecessary, trunk-sized cargo. Over the years He has helped me get rid of most of my baggage, ranging from the emotional weights of worry and fear to a variety of pet sins I carried far too long. He has helped me downsize considerably, just like we did the day the truck broke down.

Although everything we had originally packed on our bike was carefully selected in anticipation of its usefulness, we had to *reevaluate* our load. Yes, we could have made the trip with all our stuff, but we would have been miserable. We would have bottomed out for sure, and the bike would have never found its "sweet spot." Unnecessary burdens keep us from finding the groove of life we were meant to ride in.

I am learning that throughout our journey there's always something else to get rid of to lighten our load. Even now, I am aware of something from my past that God wants me to throw aside. There is no room on this trip for anything *unneces-sary*—no matter how small we think it is.

Just as God provided Allen and me with the help we needed when the truck broke down, He has provided all of us with the help we need to fix our broken lives. Colossians 2:14 in The Message says, "When you were stuck in your old sin-dead life, you were incapable of responding to God. God brought you alive—right along with Christ! Think of it! All sins forgiven, the slate wiped clean, that old arrest warrant canceled and nailed to Christ's cross."

What does God want us to do with all our unnecessary burdens and the sin that so easily trips us up? He wants us to throw them on Christ. This is what He says in 1 Peter 5:7 (AMP):

"Casting the whole of your care [all your anxieties, all your worries, all your concerns, once and for all] on Him, for He cares for you affectionately and cares about you watchfully."

Stop and listen. What is the Holy Spirit saying to you right now? What unnecessary burden is He encouraging you to get rid of? Let me say it again. We can choose to keep carrying our heavy loads, but we will be very miserable people. Trust me...I know from experience. I've been there, done that, and have several t-shirts to prove it!

Remember, God's lessons are never about Him pointing a divine finger of accusation at us. When He shows us something wrong in our lives, all He wants to do is lighten our load. In a way it's as if He is pointing to our heavy burdens and saying, "May I help you with your luggage? I can take that off your hands for ya."

Pick Up Your Mat and Walk

There is a very interesting story in John 5. Jesus was going to Jerusalem to celebrate one of the Jewish feasts. On His way, He stopped at the pool of Bethesda, a place where miraculous healings took place. The Scripture says,

"There was a certain man there who had suffered with a deep-seated and lingering disorder for thirty-eight years. When Jesus noticed him lying there [helpless], knowing that he had already been a long time in that condition, He said to him, Do you want to become well? [Are you really in earnest about getting well?]

The invalid answered, Sir, I have nobody when the water is moving to put me into the pool; but while I am trying to come [into it] myself, somebody else steps down ahead of me.

Jesus said to him, Get up! Pick up your bed (sleeping pad) and walk! Instantly the man became well and recovered his strength and picked up his bed and walked...."

—John 5:5-9 AMP

Here's a man who had been out of the game—paralyzed for thirty-eight years. Jesus basically asked, "Dude, you've been hanging out at this 'healing' pool for eons! What's the deal? Are you okay with veggin' out here, or do you really wanna get better?"

Essentially, the guy starts whining to Jesus, "I have nobody that loves me. Nobody will help me get into the pool when the water is stirred. Somebody always gets there before me." Does any of this sound familiar?

I have to say, I may be a long lost relative of this guy, as I have done my fair share of whining and feeling sorry for myself. But even in the middle of my pity parties, God has still come in and *rocked my world* just as He did the man at the pool!

I remember a time years ago when my "ride" was bottoming out. I was still carrying too much unnecessary junk in my trunk from my childhood, and the sparks were flying. Thankfully, a good friend helped God straighten me out. She saw me in my whiny condition and boldly said, "Rena, you're forty years old and still having momma issues! Get up and get over it!"

It was as if she gave me a good spiritual slap in the face. It hurt, but it was the reality check I needed. God had my attention. I wanted to go deeper in my relationship with Him, but I couldn't do it carrying all the excess baggage.

To help me grow, God connected me with someone who had dealt with some of the very same issues with their mother. He and his wife served as our adult Bible study and home group leaders for several years. They actively listened and gently counseled me. He too, gave me a slap of reality when he told me I needed to stop playing the *victim* and take my rightful position as a *victor* in Christ.

Ouch! No one had ever told me that before. Although his words stung, he was able to deliver this truth without offending me. We had developed a relationship, and I had learned to trust him. We talked a while longer and then he asked me what God was speaking to my heart. The answer rose from deep within me, "He is telling me to pick up my mat and walk." That's when this passage in John 5 came into play.

The bottom line is we all must come to a point where we get up and get over it. No more blame shifting. No more whining. No more playing the victim. We must come to Christ, own our behavior, and act upon what He is telling us. We must let go of our past and boldly walk forward into our future with Him.

REASONS WE WON'T LET GO

By now I believe you are beginning to realize the impact of what God has done. He has given us His Son, Jesus, and Jesus has given us His all. We no longer have to carry the heavy burdens of sin and all the unnecessary weights of hurt we hold on to.

Still, in our humanness, our flesh sometimes comes up with countless reasons to hold on to our baggage. Although we can't cover them all, here are six big reasons you should be aware of.

REASON #1

"I'M THE ONLY ONE."

This line of thought is one of the biggest lies we swallow. We think, *No one could possibly know where I am coming from because I am the only one with these issues.* But that's not true, and God's Word confirms it saying,

> **"No test or temptation that comes your way is beyond the course of what others have had to face. All you need to remember is that God will never let you down; he'll never let you be pushed**

past your limit; he'll always be there to help you come through it."

—1 Corinthians 10:13 The Message

And...

"Stand firm against him {*Satan*}, and be strong in your faith. Remember that your Christian brothers and sisters all over the world are going through the same kind of suffering you are."

—1 Peter 5:9 NLT
Italicized word in brackets added for clarity.

So you are not alone in your struggles. Your burdens aren't as special as you might think. There are fellow believers all over the world dealing with similar issues. Instead of thinking, *Woe is me*, thank God He is with you to help you come through it.

REASON #2

"I HAVE TO EARN GOD'S FORGIVENESS."

Many people mistakenly think we need to earn our salvation and forgiveness of sin. Even some Christians slip back into this line of thinking. As a result, they try to be "good enough" before they come to God to ask for forgiveness. They try to clean up their act and *then* come to God. This makes for a miserable existence. I know...I have done it.

Don't swallow the lie that you need to feel like crud for a while and then you can ask God to forgive you. There is nothing you can do to earn His salvation or keep your salvation. Jesus paid it all and there is nothing else that is required. God's Word says,

> **"Saving is all his idea, and all his work. All we do is trust him enough to let him do it. It's God's gift from start to finish! We don't play the major role. If we did, we'd probably go around bragging that we'd done the whole thing! No, we neither make nor save ourselves. God does both the making and saving."**
>
> **—Ephesians 2:8-9 The Message**

> **"And now, *just as you accepted* Christ Jesus as your Lord, you must continue to follow him."**
>
> **—Colossians 2:6 NLT**

So how do we *get* saved? By God's grace and mercy. How do we *stay* saved and receive forgiveness for sins after salvation? The same way—by God's grace and mercy. All we are to do is to confess our sins to God and repent—turn away from wrong and pursue what's right. He will be faithful every time to forgive us and cleanse us from all unrighteousness (see 1 John 1:9).

REASON #3

"I'M GONNA GET EVEN WITH THEM!"

I've learned that when you plan to get even with someone, you are only letting that person continue to hurt you, and the pain never dies. The hurts that we hold so tightly to, end up turning into bitterness, hatred and resentment. These are all burdens we were never meant to carry. What does God's Word say?

"Do not judge, and you will not be judged. Do not condemn, and you will not be condemned. Forgive, and you will be forgiven."

—Luke 6:37 NIV

"Don't insist on getting even; that's not for you to do. 'I'll do the judging,' says God. 'I'll take care of it.'"

—Romans 12:19 The Message

Don't play the judge; that's God's role. Forgive, and you will be forgiven. I know some people may have really done you wrong. I can totally relate, because I too have been hurt. I know it is no walk in the park to let go of the injustices done to us. But holding the hurt only hurts you. Let it go. At the very least, pray and say, "God *I want to want* to forgive..." and say the person's name. If you humbly ask for His help, He will give it.

REASON #4

"I'M AFRAID OF NOT BEING IN CONTROL."

Are we really ever in control? The truth is, you and I are not in control of the people and most of the situations around us. Trying to be in control of things will not alleviate fear—it will only perpetuate it. There are some things in life we can change, and with God's grace and wisdom we should. His Word says,

"If any of you needs wisdom to know what you should do, you should ask God, and he will give it to you. God is generous to everyone and doesn't find fault with them."

—James 1:5 GW

When questions arise, run to God and ask Him for wisdom to know what to do. He has promised to "...guide you along the best pathway for your life..." (Psalm 32:8 NLT). If He shows you that you have no control over the situation, receive His peace and do not be afraid. He says,

"Fear not [there is nothing to fear], for I am with you; do not look around you in terror and be dismayed, for I am your God. I will strengthen and harden you to difficulties, yes, I will help you; yes, I will hold you up and retain you with My [victorious] right hand of rightness and justice."

—Isaiah 41:10 AMP

Give up the burden of trying to control everything. It only serves to make you sick. Seek God for wisdom and be at peace in the process.

REASON #5

"I NEED TO PROTECT AND DEFEND MYSELF."

If you believe this lie, you are probably carrying heavy brick walls you have built in your heart over the years because you don't trust anyone. This too is an unnecessary burden. Scripture says,

"God's your Guardian, right at your side to protect you—shielding you from sunstroke, sheltering you from moonstroke. God guards you from every evil, he guards your very life. He guards you when you leave and when you return, he guards you now, he guards you always."

—Psalm 121:5-8 The Message

Yes, if you get rid of your walls, you will be vulnerable to hurt. But you will also be open to love. You have to let your guard down in order to truly love and be loved. Surrender your life to God daily and let Him be your Guardian. Continue to pray for Him to heal you of past hurts by revealing His incredible, limitless love. As your understanding of His love is perfected, or made complete, fear will be cast out (see 1 John 4:18).

REASON #6

"I DON'T KNOW HOW TO ACT OR WHO I AM WITHOUT MY BURDENS."

It's true that after holding on to your burdens for a long time, they often become intertwined with your identity. Sure, they have served their purpose of keeping others at a safe distance, but they have outlived their usefulness. *In Christ* you have been given a new identity. He says,

"For if a man {*or woman*} is in Christ he becomes a new person altogether—the past is finished and gone, everything has become fresh and new."

—2 Corinthians 5:17 PHILLIPS
Italicized words in brackets added for clarity.

Remember my "searching and *fearless* moral inventory of myself," from Lesson 5? I had pages and pages of stuff to let go of. You may be in the same boat. I know it's going be tough to let go, but with God's grace you can surely give these things to Him.

In exchange, He will begin to paint a picture on your heart of your new identity in Him. He says you are the *righteousness of God* in Christ Jesus. You are the *apple of His eye*. You are *chosen and approved of* since before you were born. You are *more than a conqueror* in Him and so much more![2]

"REMIND ME, PLEASE"

Once we learn these kinds of truths and quit believing the enemy's lies, we still have to be reminded of them from time to time.

Allen did this for me one Valentine's Day. I had just reinjured my lower back after making some progress in my recovery from surgery. I was in pain almost constantly and taking the maximum amount of medication prescribed—just to lie in bed. Once again, I had become a real hag and hard to get along with.

During this time we started our *Love and Respect* home fellowship, using Dr. Eggrichs' materials. The people in our group often spoke about what God had shown me—that some of us have a lot more baggage to work through than others. Instead of us starting from a *blue* and *pink* perspective as Dr. Eggrichs suggests, we started from *black* and *red*.

As a result of my increased physical pain and other challenges, I was really struggling with some anger issues again and began entertaining the lie, "You're never going to fully get this...You're always going to be struggling with anger."

Thankfully, my husband had been doing his homework. On Valentine's Day morning I woke up to a single pink rose and a handwritten note that read, "You don't have to be red anymore!" What a wonderful reminder, and he was so right!

He was gently reminding me that I had already been set free from a victim mentality. I did not have to continue carrying anger or self-defeat any longer. With Allen's reminder, I gladly laid it back down at the foot of the cross where it belonged. I started having a better attitude almost instantly.

But, there was a time when I didn't let go of my burdens so easily as this. I was afraid of what it would be like to not have all the dysfunction and chaos in my life. Thank God, my never ending list of reasons for not letting go have all been shot down. They just can't stand up to the truth of God's Word. He says,

> **"Fear not; you will no longer live in shame. Don't be afraid; there is no more disgrace for you. You will no longer remember the shame of your youth and the sorrows of widowhood."**
>
> **—Isaiah 54:4 NLT**

Remember, any reason for holding onto unnecessary burdens is a lie from the devil meant to keep you in bondage. How can you know if you're holding something you need to get rid of? The answer is, what kind of fruit is it producing in your life? If it is *not* producing things like love, joy, peace, kindness, patience and self-control, which are the fruits of God's Spirit,[3] it is probably something you need to get rid of. As you stop believing the enemy's lies and surrender your burdens to God, you will experience the awesome benefits of letting go.

THE BENEFITS OF LETTING GO ARE GREAT!

Psalm 103:2 (AMP) says, "Bless (affectionately, gratefully praise) the Lord, O my soul, and forget not [one of] all His benefits...."

There are more benefits of "letting go and letting God" take care of you than time or space allows. Nevertheless, you need to know that relinquishing your burdens releases God's peace, joy, and genuine love into our lives.

It also gives God glory. Think about it. If you have peace, joy and love in your heart, it's going to show on your face and in your attitude. People are going to be drawn to you. They will want what you have, and eventually they will ask you about it. What an opportunity to share the truth and love of Jesus!

Which brings me to what I believe is the greatest reason we need to throw off unnecessary burdens and that is **to help others**. Look around you. There are people everywhere who are hurting and in desperate need of help. We have what they need—a relationship with Jesus Christ.

The farmer that we "accidentally" found the day our truck broke down didn't just help us, we helped him. He was an Iraqi veteran trying desperately to keep his family's farm afloat. We had the opportunity to encourage him, bless him financially, and pray with him before we left. God spoke to his heart and showed him that He was aware of their struggles and that He would help them make it through.

When we seek to be in God's will, nothing is ever just for us. As God blessed Abraham to be a blessing to others, so He has blessed us to be a blessing to others (see Genesis 12:1-3). There is always someone who can benefit from what we have learned and experienced.

I wish I could say that Allen and I have always been sensitive and successful in reaching out to others, but we haven't. There were times in the past when we were too busy holding onto our burdens to reach out and help others in need. It's called a missed opportunity, and no one can see the grace of God in our lives when this happens.

God has set us free from so many things, and He wants us to live in that freedom. He doesn't want us walking around like we still have a huge tumor on our side after He has already removed it. On the contrary, He wants us to "Be ready at any time to give a quiet and reverent answer to any man who wants a reason for the hope that you have within you" (1 Peter 3:15 PHILLIPS).

My prayer for you when things go wrong is that you are quick to repent and get things right between you, God and others. Don't hold on to any unnecessary burden Christ died to set you free from, and don't go back to wallow in the pit of self-pity He has pulled you out of. Confess your sins, repent of your ways, receive His forgiveness, and go on. "Pile your troubles on God's shoulders—he'll carry your load, he'll help you out..." (Psalm 55:22 The Message).

Lesson Summary

Something to Hold On To

Jesus carried our burdens and nailed them to the cross so that we don't have to carry them any longer. It's really that simple. First Peter 2:24 (NLT) says, "He personally carried our sins in his body on the cross so that we can be dead to sin and live for what is right. By his wounds you are healed."

God wants you to cast all your unnecessary burdens on Jesus. He wants you to lean on Him and trust Him to be your helper in all areas of your life. You have a brand new identity in Christ Jesus. So strip off and throw aside every *unnecessary weight* and the *sin* that so readily clings to and entangles you. Run with patient endurance the race that is marked out for you. In Christ, you are destined to win!

Rena's playlist:

- "Forgiven" ~ by Sanctus Real

- "Remind Me Who I Am" ~ by Jason Gray

- "Let It Go" ~ by Tenth Avenue North

- "The Hurt and the Healer" ~ by Mercy Me

- "Steady My Heart" ~ by Kari Jobe

Questions for personal or group reflection:

- What things do you tend to worry about? Carefully read Matthew 6:25-34; Psalm 34:9-10; 84:11; and 2 Corinthians 9:8-11. What is God showing you in these verses about *not* worrying?

- Stop and listen. What is the Holy Spirit saying to you right now? What unnecessary burden(s) is He encouraging you to let go of? Write them and release them to God in prayer.

- Of all the reasons presented for not releasing unnecessary burdens, which one(s) do you identify with most? Explain why and tell how this lesson has helped free you from these lies.

- What is your greatest "take away" from this lesson— what came alive and jumped off the pages that you want to remember?

---

[1] Lisa Bevere, *Out of Control and Loving It!* (Lake Mary, FL: Charisma House, 2006) p. 12.
[2] See 2 Corinthians 5:21; Zechariah 2:8; Jeremiah 1:5; Romans 8:37.
[3] See Galatians 5:22-23.

"Where does your security lie? Is God your refuge, your hiding place, your stronghold, your shepherd, your counselor, your friend, your redeemer, your saviour, your guide? If He is, you don't need to search any further for security."

—Elisabeth Elliot[1]

Lesson 7

Finding
the Right Seat

*And He raised us up together with Him and made us sit
down together [giving us joint seating with Him] in the
heavenly sphere [by virtue of our being] in Christ Jesus
(the Messiah, the Anointed One).*

Ephesians 2:6 AMP

For several years I wasn't able to ride with Allen much
at all. After years of chronic pain, I finally had two discs
removed and three vertebrae fused in my neck. The
surgery went as planned with great results...until I jammed

my head into the doorframe of my blazer six weeks after the operation.

That incident started a year of reinjuring my neck again and again. Over the next nine months, I experienced many minor injuries. Then I fell off my daughter's horse, resulting in whiplash. After completing a course of physical therapy for this injury, I had a head on collision. I have struggled physically ever since then.

Many days I found myself horizontal more hours than vertical. It seemed like an eternity before I was able to ride again. Smooth rides around the block strained my neck and shoulders, but hitting small bumps would wipe me out up to a couple of weeks.

During this time we trailered our 2000 Heritage Springer, the one we bought salvaged in Virginia, to Abernathy's Harley-Davidson in Tennessee. After test driving several of their bikes, we traded the Springer for a 2006 Heritage Softail Classic. She was cobalt blue, and Allen named her *Rebekah*.

This was our very first brand new motorcycle after wrenching on older bikes for over twenty-five years. We not only chose it for its looks, but also for the way it rode. For the first time, we were considering the season of life we were in and the days ahead. I think that meant we were growing up.

Bums Away!

When it came time for Rebekah's 10,000 mile check-up, Allen made an appointment with her homeboys back at Abernathy's. Of course, this meant another road trip, so we took advantage of the opportunity and invited some friends along for the ride.

The day we were to leave couldn't have been more perfect. I was really looking forward to a nice day of riding and fellowship, but dreading it at the same time. Both feelings were based on one little bit of information; It was going to be the longest ride I had been on in years. Since I hadn't been in the saddle for quite some time, a certain part of my anatomy had lost its endurance. Okay, I won't be shy about it. It was my rear end.

Unfortunately, after our thirty minute putt to meet everyone, I was already in pain. I welcomed the short break for breakfast, but it was too short. Before I knew it we were saddled up again and headed to Tennessee—all seven bikes and riders.

After about an hour, I was in need of relief. I had gone full circle, trying several different seating positions. There were only so many I could choose from. I even sat on things not made for sitting. By this point, Allen started to get a clue. He patted my leg and kindly asked, "Do you need a break? You want to pull over?"

With a stiff upper lip I declined the offer. "No, keep going." Then I got in my "go to" position, carefully wrapping my legs around his waist.

When you ride with the "big boys," especially those who are hard core, long-distance riders, you don't want to be the one who causes everyone to have to stop before someone's gas tank is thirsty. Thankfully, one of the guys needed gas just about the time I was ready to scream.

Allen strategically pulled into a truck stop, thinking we might find something "cushy for my tushy." Peeling myself off the seat, I waddled to the restroom. I nearly cried when I realized I was going to have to sit on the toilet. But I sucked it up like a big girl and did what was necessary.

When I had finally gotten myself together, I found Allen feverishly looking for something that would soften the ride for me. *Wow, I love that man!* The only thing we could find that might work was a bright yellow squishy pillow stuffed with tiny foam pellets. Hugging it tightly, knowing we would shortly become quite intimate; I took my new best friend up to the counter and joined the guys who were paying for their gas and coffee.

One of them looked down at me holding my squishy cushy. Seeing I had a grimace on my face, he asked, "You okay, Sis?"

I blurted out the only thing that came to mind, "All I can say is that's the first time since I was a little girl that I wanted to pee standing up." I guess that was 'nuff said. He just smiled and patted me gently on the head.

Back at the now perceived "torture apparatus on wheels," I was hopeful that we had found the remedy for what ailed me. With a fresh excitement for the rest of the trip, I proudly placed my pillow in its place of prominence and carefully climbed back on.

My excitement immediately gave way the moment my bum hit the pillow. All of the squishies squished right out from under my sore parts. There was no time to re-adjust it because as soon as I was on the bike Allen peeled out. With about two more hours of hard riding ahead of us, I did the only thing I knew to do: pray and attempt to stuff squishes back into place. I prayed, shifted positions and then prayed some more the rest of the way there.

I was so happy to reach our destination that I started getting off the bike before Allen had stopped. Although he was not ready for me to bail just yet, he did manage to keep her upright...but not without a few grumbles directed my way. Please don't try this at home, folks.

It's Just a Loaner

With Rebekah signed in for her "spa day," everyone was ready to get some lunch. By this time, I could have gone without getting on another bike for the rest of the riding season. Reluctantly, I slowly eased onto the 2004 Ultra Classic the repair shop had loaned us while waiting for ours to be serviced. Surprisingly, I relaxed in its plushness and was able to rest on its seat.

I gave it my all trying to talk Allen into giving up our new bike for one similar to the loaner. But as we sat at a stoplight with every joint in our bodies vibrating with the engine, we remembered why we had decided against these kinds of bikes when we bought our little Becky. Neither of us cares for the way the rubber motor mounts vibrate when idling. We love the comfort and ride while accelerating, but not enough to own one.

For the first time since I could remember, Allen was content with our current bike and didn't want to change. He was, however, hip to checking out a new seat. So as soon as we got back to the shop after lunch, we beat feet over to the seat display. After carefully studying all the options, we learned that none of the plush seats were made to fit on Softails. I was extremely bummed!

By then we were informed that Rebekah's "mileage makeover" was complete. We paid the bill and hit the road for home. With my bum a bit more rested, the ride started off feeling much better. But all too soon I was hurting again—*way* too soon for my liking. Thankfully, Allen figured out a way to contain my yellow squishy pillow inside my hoody during one of our stops. With it tightly bound, it stayed where it was supposed to for the remainder of the trip.

The rest of the way home, we were both pretty slap happy and numbly laughing. It was a sweet change from just a few years earlier—years when neither of us would have liked the other very much by that point in the trip. That's what stress will do when we let it get to us. But God had brought about change in our character, and that change was wonderfully welcomed!

FINDING SWEET FAVOR
WITH MY BEST FRIEND

Once we made it home, I informed Allen that I would not be able to ride with him on a regular basis if I was going to be in that much pain. To my surprise, he turned to me and very sweetly said, "I won't be riding much longer either if you aren't going to be riding with me."

I was blown away! What a sacrificial position he was taking. Just the thought of it melted my heart. It was all I needed to know his love for me had genuinely grown into more than I could have dreamed. It was a far cry from the days I chased him down the driveway throwing rocks at him as he peeled out on his bike without me.

The next day I knew without a doubt his response was sincere. He began doing everything he could to make our bike comfortable for me. He worked on it for weeks, experimenting with many different seats but to no avail. He then stuffed some extra foam padding into the best seat he could find, added a new backrest, and strapped on an armrest to a new tour pack.

His effort paid off! The new accessories made a huge difference. The biggest difference I noticed, however, was my man's amazing attitude of love. We had come a long way in our ride together. No, our marriage wasn't completely smooth, but we sure were on the right road.

Not too long ago, the Lord reminded me of a specific prayer I prayed for myself during the time when our relationship was extremely bumpy. I had pleaded with God to give me favor with my husband. I asked Him for the same favor He had given Esther with King Ahasuerus in the Old Testament. Scripture says,

> **"And the king loved Esther more than all the women, and she obtained grace and** *favor* **in his sight more than all the maidens, so that he set the royal crown on her head and made her queen instead of Vashti."**
>
> **—Esther 2:17 AMP**

My sisters, I pray this encourages you. If your relationship feels like it's about to bite the dust, pray! God truly does hear your cries and will answer your prayers as they line up with His will. He has surely answered mine, and what He did for me and others, He will do for you. "For God does not show favoritism" (Romans 2:11 NLT). He wants your marriage to thrive. I now have awesome favor with my husband and have no doubts of his love for me.

A DEMONSTRATION OF REAL LOVE

Several years after our trip to Tennessee, some friends loaned us their Airhawk motorcycle cushion to try. What an invention! For those who don't know, these cushions are constructed in the same way as wheel chair cushions. They have small air bladders that can be made firmer or softer, depending on your need.

We had planned on putting this cushion to the test on our dream trip to Colorado—the same trip I've mentioned in three previous lessons. While Allen was loading the bike onto the trailer the day before we were to leave, he realized the cushion was missing. Frantically, we searched high and low, tearing through the garage, the house, the truck and the car. It was nowhere to be found.

I was shaking in my little "Harley boots" as panic tried to grip me, but I chose to not give in to fear. Allen, on the other hand, was beside himself. I repeatedly told him, "Don't worry about it. It's going to be ok." I was determined that this wasn't going to be an issue in any way.

After fervent prayer, he began calling all the local Harley shops, but not one of them carried Airhawk cushions. He then decided to research the manufacturer to see where the closest shop was that carried Airhawk products. As closing time was fast approaching, he found a distributor about an hour away. The bummer was it was in the opposite direction of our destination. This made no difference to my man. He would not deny me what I needed to make the trip in as much comfort as possible. He made arrangements to purchase the "life saver" for my bottom when the factory opened the next day.

The following morning we left two hours earlier than planned to allot for the extra miles. All this just for me, and not once did my husband even give a hint of complaining. In fact, he did just the opposite. I have to tell you, part of me felt like a royal pain in the rumpus. It was hard for me to accept his gift of kindness without feeling guilty and undeserving of all his extra effort. His actions were Christ-like—a demonstration of real love.

Later that day, I found out why that cushion was so important. As I mentioned in Lesson 6, the truck broke down four hours outside of our friend's home, forcing us to leave it and the trailer prematurely. This unfortunate turn of events caused us to have to ride the bike an extra 200 miles. I can't begin to express to you how grateful I was to have that cushion. Having the right seat is priceless!

Road Trippin' with Jesus... He Gives Us the Best Seats

This whole trip and seat scenario really got me thinking. My husband's genuine love was hard to receive. I still had the mentality that I didn't deserve it. Consequently, I was willing to settle for a less desirable seat than the one I needed for our trip. But because of Allen's genuine love for me and the grace of God working through his life, we had an awesome vacation—even with the extra time on the bike!

Think about it. My man went to a lot of trouble to help me find just the right seat because he loves me. Can you imagine how much more our heavenly Father, who loves us immeasurably, wants to help us find "the right seat" for our road trip with Him?

When you and I finally get to the place in our life-long journey that we are open to seeing who Jesus truly is, things begin to change. As we surrender to Him and His goodness, He opens our eyes so we can see that He's been riding with us all along. Through every season of our lives, He's been there, although we never saw it. He has been adding extra padding where we need it, while removing the fluff that keeps us separated from Him.

I looked up the word "seat" in the Bible and discovered quite a number of scriptures about how, when, where and why we sit. In one version there are sixty-four references. Out of everything that's presented, there are five areas I feel are worthy of our attention, starting with the place where Jesus is seated right now.

JESUS' SEAT

To understand where Jesus is seated, we must first understand why He came. In the beginning, God created men and women to be in fellowship with Him. He walked and talked with Adam "in the cool of the day" in the Garden of Eden. They were friends. But Adam and Eve sinned; they disobeyed God and as a result, the relationship between God and man was broken. Mankind, in our fallen, sinful state, could not restore our connection. Only God could reconnect us in relationship with Himself, and He did it through Jesus, His Son. Here's the deal on how it went down.

God became flesh and was born as baby Jesus (see John 1:10-18). Jesus grew up staying under the "seat of authority" of His parents until the age of thirty. At that time He started His ministry here on earth, lasting approximately three years. Everything Jesus said and did was what He saw God the Father say and do (see John 5:19-20). He lived a sinless life and then laid His life down, dying a criminal's death on a cross.

Though He was innocent, He chose to die in our place. Carrying our sin, guilt and shame upon Himself, He paid a debt He did not owe—the debt we could not pay. But Jesus did not stay dead. Three days after He was crucified, God's Holy Spirit raised Him back to life! For forty days, He was not only seen by His eleven remaining disciples but also by hundreds of others—Scripture says over 500 at one time (see 1 Corinthians 15:3-8).

Where is He now? The Bible says God "...raised Him from the dead and seated Him at His [own] right hand in the heavenly [places]" (Ephesians 1:20 AMP). This seating of our Savior was also foretold by the prophet Daniel. He said, "As I looked, 'thrones were set in place, and the Ancient of Days took his seat...'" (7:9 NIV). Jesus Himself prophesied where He would be declaring, "But from now on, the Son of Man will be seated at the right hand of the mighty God" (Luke 22:69 NIV).

Through Jesus' death and resurrection, He overcame death, hell and the grave, taking His appointed seat at the right hand of the Father. Why would a perfect God enter a wicked world, take the form of frail flesh, and die a criminal's death to pay a debt He did not owe? One reason...Love. "God **loved** the people of this world so much that he gave his only Son, so that everyone who has faith in him will have eternal life and never really die" (John 3:16 CEV).

I did not understand any of this until I surrendered my life to God and allowed Him to *sit* on the throne of my heart. At that time my spiritual eyes were opened and I began to understand His limitless love. For the first time I believed Jesus died *for me.* How do we know that we know God loves us? "God demonstrates his own love for us in this: While we were still sinners, Christ died for us" (Romans 5:8 NIV).

This may be hard for you to grasp. I know; it was for me too. The fact that Jesus could die for me while I hated Him and was so ugly on the inside is truly unbelievable. But He did it—not just for me, but for you too.

You may be feeling a tug on your heart at this very moment. Tears may be on the brink of cascading down your face. Don't hold back. That's God's Holy Spirit right there present with you, drawing you to the Father! If you have never surrendered your life to Him or have wandered away from His friendship, take time now to make things right. Ask Him to forgive you of your sins and to sit on the throne of your heart. There is a prayer you can pray inviting Him into your life on page 187 if you need a little help.

WHERE WE *SHOULD* SIT

Once we surrender our lives to God, inviting Jesus into our heart and trusting Him with our lives, we are given a brand new seat. That seat is **in Christ**. Spiritually speaking, where He is seated, we are seated. Again, the Scripture says,

"...{*God*} raised Him from the dead and seated him at his right hand in the heavenly realms, far above all rule and authority, power and dominion, and every title that can be given, not only in the present age but also in the one to come. And God placed all things under his feet and appointed him to be head over everything for the church.

"And God raised us up with Christ and seated us with him in the heavenly realms in Christ Jesus, in order that in the coming ages he might show the incomparable riches of his grace, expressed in his kindness to us in Christ Jesus."

—**Ephesians 1:20-22; 2:6-7 NIV**
Italicized word in brackets added for clarity.

Did you catch that? Spiritually, you and I are seated *in Christ* in heavenly places. We are far above all the power of the enemy and this world. Everything that is under Jesus' feet is under our feet. This is a powerful truth that God wants us to know and believe.

As I shared in Lesson 1, I lived on the streets as a teenager. Many times I woke up with a hangover or still drunk in places like cemeteries, piles of dirty laundry, and even a ditch behind an old log. My life was such a shattered mess I didn't believe anything good about myself or feel I deserved anything good for a very long time. But God's Word is true regardless of our feelings.

Scripture says, "He lifted me out of the ditch, pulled me from deep mud. He stood me up on a solid rock to make sure I wouldn't slip" (Psalm 40:2, The Message). And in 1 Samuel 2:8 (NLT) it says, "He lifts the poor from the dust and the needy from the garbage dump. He sets them among princes, placing them in **seats of honor**. For all the earth is the Lord's, and he has set the world in order." Wow! What a priceless privilege we have been given! A seat of honor in Christ!

Dear Friends, please don't follow your feelings. They lie. Truth trumps feelings. Choose to believe what God says in His Word over how you feel. If you have surrendered your life to Him, you are now seated in Christ in a place of honor—not because of anything you have or haven't done, but because of everything Jesus did!

Take Your Seat in His Church

Where and how we sit in the natural realm is also important. Instead of spending my time casually sitting at the bar like I used to, I now actively sit amongst the body of Christ in my home church. It's where I belong. And there is a place in the local church for you, too.

For many of us, the first time we visit a church can be extremely awkward. I still remember my first visit. Once I got past the front doors and the walls didn't cave in, I was clueless about what to do next. I didn't know how I fit in or even where to sit, literally. Have ya been there?

If you haven't found your seat in the local church or have tried and for whatever reason it wasn't a good experience, please don't be afraid to try again. Take it easy on yourself. Give yourself a chance to do some "test driving." Continue checking out different churches to find the seat that is best for you. It may take time to see where God wants you to cop a squat.

When you decide to give church a try, look for a smiling face to help you. If you don't find someone right away, that's okay. Go to the next person until you find someone eager to show you to your seat. I pray God will lead you to the person just for you, who will ask you to sit with them while you get comfortable.

Symbolically, your seat in a healthy, Bible-believing church is a seat at Jesus' feet. Next to spending personal time in God's presence, reading the Word and praying, there is no "sweeter spot." Mary, the sister of Martha, chose this place. What did Jesus say about Mary's choice? "There is only one thing worth being concerned about. Mary has discovered it, and it will not be taken away from her" (Luke 10:42 NLT).

Sitting at Jesus' feet is the one thing worth being concerned about. It puts us in our "right mind." Luke confirms this explaining what happened to the demon-possessed man: "...When they came to Jesus, they found the man from whom the demons had gone out, **sitting at Jesus' feet**, dressed and in his *right mind*..." (Luke 8:35 NIV).

I assure you there is a special place set just for you in God's Church, the body of Christ, and the local church God leads you to. No one else can fill the seat at Jesus' feet that is meant for you. Find your seat and fill it.

WHERE WE SHOULD *NOT* SIT

Just like the multiple motorcycle seats I tried to sit on but couldn't get comfortable, there are also a number of seats where we are *not* meant to sit in the body of Christ. The one I want to focus on is the seat of pride—a place where we think of ourselves more highly than we should.

Jesus gives us an example of this seat in His frequent run-ins with the Pharisees. If anyone had a problem with pride and self-importance, it was them. Jesus said,

> **"Everything they do is done for people to see: They make their phylacteries[2] wide and the tassels on their garments long; they love the place of honor at banquets and the most important seats in the synagogues; they love to be greeted with respect in the marketplaces and to be called 'Rabbi' by others."**

> **—Matthew 23:5-7 NIV**

And in the Gospel of Luke, Jesus said,

> **"Woe to you Pharisees, because you love the most important seats in the synagogues and greetings in the marketplaces. Woe to you, because you are like unmarked graves, which men walk over without knowing it."**

> **—Luke 11:43-44 NIV**

Wow! Talk about telling it like it is. Jesus never softened His words or stance when it came to religious pride. He hated it, and we should too. This reminds me of a time recently when I was asked to serve as a leader in a class at our church.

Allen and I sat in a "new beginnings" Sunday school class as we went through two different books filled with Christianity 101 lessons. It was a great class that God used to lay a solid foundation of basic biblical truths. It was also a place where we could be real and ask any and all of our questions. Sitting in this class was key to our growth and walk with the Lord. If you don't have a class like this at the church you're attending, talk to your pastor about starting one.

Allen and I completed this class over twenty years ago. Since then, I have often begged our new Christian friends to attend it so I can go with them. Well one day someone said yes to my request. It was my mom. She had rededicated her life to the Lord and was starting life afresh. I attended the class with her to help her feel more comfortable. I was filled with joy over her new commitment to Christ and at the same time delighted to have an excuse to go to Sunday school with her.

When my mom and her husband went back to Texas for the winter, I expected to move on to a different class until she returned the following summer. Much to my surprise, one of the leaders asked me to stay to help in the class. It was our long-time friend C.R. Kersten, who also serves as director of the St. Louis Men's Teen Challenge outreach. He told me that he would talk with the necessary people but felt there wouldn't be any problem.

I told him, "If God wants me to, I would be happy to do it. But I don't want to try to make it happen." I knew in my heart if the seat was for me, no one else could sit in it and be comfy. I also knew that I would never be comfortable if it was meant for someone else. With this mind set, I gave the situation to God and left it with Him where it belonged. I played it cool, planning to not bring it up myself ever again.

However, when I ran into C.R. a few weeks later, he brought it up. He told me how he had spoken to one person in authority, and they said it was fine. He still needed to clear it with someone else though. At that point, I shared with him the fear that crippled me every time I tried to step out in faith—the fear of making mistakes and failing miserably.

Our friend C.R. very transparently began to tell me of the mistakes he had made in his earlier years of ministry. I was blessed to tears as he encouraged me by humbling himself. He was helping me to find my new "right seat" in the church—not by sharing his victories but his failures. Bless God! I am now one of the helpers in this most awesome class! God made it happen! Now He gets all the glory for the good that comes out of it.

Friends, let's take to heart the instruction God gives us through the apostle Paul:

"...I warn everyone among you not to estimate and think of himself more highly than he ought [not to have an exaggerated opinion of his own importance], but to rate his ability with sober

judgment, each according to the degree of faith apportioned by God to him."

—Romans 12:3 AMP

The temptation to elevate yourself in the eyes of others will come, but don't give in to it. Seek the *seat of service and influence* that God has for you. There you will find joy, peace and fulfillment.

THE JUDGMENT SEAT

There is one seat mentioned in the Bible that we will never sit in. Instead, we will stand before it. It's the Judgment Seat of Christ. Romans 14:10 (KJV) says, "...For we shall all stand before the judgment seat of Christ." The J. B. Phillips translation of this verse says, "...We shall all be judged one day, not by each other's standards or even our own, but by the standard of Christ." Wow! What a sobering thought.

Many years ago the Lord gave me a dream. In the dream I was going up a hill, and all along the hillside were terraces of graves with tombstones. At the top of the hill there were people, all of whom were in ministry, doing a victory dance. The Lord revealed to me that these people's ministries had been built on death; the graves represented people who had been left behind spiritually wounded on their way to the top. How sad is that?

The reality is people will get hurt from time to time by things that we say or do. Many times it is totally accidental. It happens and is a part of life. Nonetheless, we are left with a choice: take time to care for them and help them heal or leave them for dead and move on. May I suggest the Golden Rule: "Do to others as you would like them to do to you" (Luke 6:31 NLT).

God did not show me that dream so that I would judge the leaders in ministry. He showed me the dream so that I would judge my own heart and actions, allowing Him to expose my true motives. I am responsible for me, and you are responsible for you.

"Yes, each of us will give a personal account to God" (Romans 14:12 NLT). Again, "...we must all appear before the judgment seat of Christ, that each one may receive what is due him for the things done while in the body, whether good or bad" (2 Corinthians 5:10 NIV). Let's let Christ be the Judge. If we give mercy, we will receive mercy.

THE MERCY SEAT

The last seat I want to look at is my favorite! It is God's mercy seat. The first mention of God's mercy seat is in the Old Testament—Exodus 25:15-22. God gave detailed directions to Moses for building the tabernacle, the place where He, Himself would dwell. The tabernacle was like a portable church that could be set up and taken down wherever the people of Israel went. In this tabernacle were furnishings that God considered holy. The mercy seat was one of them, and it was actually a part of the Ark of the Covenant. God told Moses,

"And you shall make a mercy seat (a covering) of pure gold.... There I will meet with you and, from above the mercy seat, from between the two cherubim that are upon the ark of the Testimony,

I will speak intimately with you of all which I will give you in commandment to the Israelites."

—Exodus 25:17, 22 AMP

According to the law God gave Moses and the people of Israel, there had to be a blood sacrifice to cover the people's sins. These animal sacrifices were performed by priests and then offered to God in prayer. The blood was then placed on the mercy seat.

"And put the incense on the fire [in the censer] before the Lord, that the cloud of the incense may cover the mercy seat that is upon [the ark of] the Testimony... 14He shall take of the bull's blood and sprinkle it with his finger on the front [the east side] of the mercy seat...."

—Leviticus 16:13-14 AMP

When the animal died, it symbolically took the place of the people. Its life is in its blood, so its life was given to cover the sins of the people. This was a foretelling of what God was going to do for all of mankind through Jesus.

In the Gospels we find the story of His life, death and resurrection. He became a sacrifice to end all sacrifices for our sins. But His blood doesn't just cover our sins—it *takes our sins away* (see Hebrews 10:3-4; 10-12.) Praise God! That is the Good News!

Keep in mind, "the wages of sin is death, but the free gift of God is eternal life through Christ Jesus our Lord" (Romans 6:23 NLT). Jesus paid the wages for our sin. He fulfilled the law. He is our Mercy!

"[All] are justified and made upright and in right standing with God, freely and gratuitously by His grace (His unmerited favor and mercy), through the redemption which is [provided] in Christ Jesus, Whom God put forward [before the eyes of all] as a mercy seat and propitiation by His blood [the cleansing and life-giving sacrifice of atonement and reconciliation, to be received] through faith...."

—Romans 3:24-25 AMP

God's mercy is truly incredible. That's where I want to hang out! Because of His mercy, we have salvation through Jesus. Because of His mercy, we are not destroyed. Thank God His "...mercy triumphs over judgment!" (James 2:13 NIV) "Great is his faithfulness; his mercies begin afresh each morning" (Lamentations 3:23 NLT).

Friends, I invite you to taste and see that God is good! Run to Jesus, your Mercy Seat. Fellowship with Him by sitting at His feet. As you surrender your life to Him, He will give you just the right seat for the ride of your life!

Lesson Summary

Something to Hold On To

There are many seats that we will sit in throughout the seasons of our lives. We all begin sitting under the authority of our parents. We then move to the position of student, wife, and mother, all the way to the day we stand before the Judgment Seat of Christ.

I pray that God will give you grace to not despise the seat He has you positioned in at this moment. These are the places God uses to prepare us for our future seats. The best seat is the one He currently has you in, not seats in your past or the ones in your future. Don't strive to get to the next seat before its appointed time. Every change of season will bring its own opportunities.

Just as I rested in the seat of the loaner bike, you and I can learn to rest and relax in our appropriate seats at the appropriate times if we don't get too big for our britches. The choice is up to us whether we will whine or shine through the changes. From this point on, let's make up our minds to never again settle for anything less than God's best, and He will take care of the rest.

Rena's playlist:

- "Every Season" ~ by Nichole Nordeman

- "You Lead" ~ by Jamie Grace

- "The Mercy Seat" ~ by Don Moen

Questions for personal or group reflection:

- Carefully reread the section "Jesus' Seat." What new things is God showing you in the summary of man's creation, fall, and redemption through Christ? How does it strengthen your faith?

- According to Ephesians 1:20-22; 2:6-7, where is Jesus seated and where are you seated as a believer? Where is the enemy? How does this encourage you? (Also check out 1 Peter 3:22; Philippians 2:9-11.)

- Why is it unwise to follow your feelings? What should you follow instead? Why?

- The Pharisees give us an example of a place *not* to sit— the seat of pride and self-importance. Ironically, it's hard to tell if we're in it. Get quiet before God and ask Him to show you your heart. Are there areas of your life where you're sitting in this seat? If so, ask Him to forgive you and give you humility.

- In what ways are you challenged by your understanding of the Judgment Seat of Christ? In what ways are you encouraged by the gift of mercy seat?

- What is your greatest "take away" from this lesson— what came alive and jumped off the pages that you want to remember?

---

[1] Quotes on *Peace with God* (http://dailychristianquote.com/ dcqpeacewithgod.html, accessed 6/8/12).
[2] Small cases enclosing certain Scripture passages, worn during prayer on the left arm and forehead.

Closing Thoughts

If there was one psalm that summed up the cry of my life, it would probably be Psalm 116. Verses 1-6 say,

"I love God because he listened to me, listened as I begged for mercy. He listened so intently as I laid out my case before him.

Death stared me in the face, hell was hard on my heels.

Up against it, I didn't know which way to turn; then I called out to God for help:

'Please, God!' I cried out. 'Save my life!'

God is gracious—it is he who makes things right, our most compassionate God.

God takes the side of the helpless; when I was at the end of my rope, he saved me."

Psalm 116:1-6 The Message

As we have journeyed together through these lessons, I pray that you have begun to see God's immense love for you and experienced His grace to help you grow up in His ways. He is ever present and ever willing to hold your hand through everything you face.

When you encounter difficulties, remember these words from Him: "Be strong and courageous. Do not be afraid or terrified because of them, for the Lord your God goes with you; he will never leave you nor forsake you" (Deuteronomy 31:6 NIV).

I know firsthand that this promise is true. God has always been with me. Even when I denied His existence and sold my soul to the enemy, He was there. Without His grace I would be dead. There is no earthly reason for me to be alive other than God has a plan for me—and He has a plan for you too!

I pray you will allow God to *Rock Your World!* May you learn that He is someone you can **always** trust. May you continue to seek His presence and saturate yourself in His truth. Although you may not see or feel Him at first, may you know in your heart that He is working in your life.

Don't waste another minute living a defeated life. See yourself as a **victor** not a victim. There is victory and freedom to be had! I leave you with these lyrics from American Idol finalist and Christian recording artist Mandisa's song "Waiting for Tomorrow." Today is the day of a new beginning!

Maybe today I'll start believing
That your mercy is really
As real as you say it is
It doesn't matter who I used to be
It only matters that I've been set free
You rescued me you're changing me
Jesus take everything
Can't live my whole life wasting
All the grace that I know You've given
Cause You've made me for so much more
Than sitting on the sidelines
I don't wanna look back and wonder
If good enough could've been better
Everyday's a day to start over
So, why am I waiting for tomorrow

Illustration A

The illustration on the next page shows how sin separates us from God (see Isaiah 59:2). This separation is common to everyone who sins. Scripture tells us that **all** have sinned and fallen short of the glory of God (see Romans 3:23).

This means even the chick or dude that you think is perfect has sinned just like you and me. In fact, anyone who relies on their good works to be made right with God (to receive salvation) is just as separated from Him as a nonbeliever who does no good works at all.

No matter how hard we try, our good works and religious practices will never bring us closer to the Father, nor will they get us into heaven. God's Word clearly declares,

"For it is by grace you have been saved, through faith—and this is not from yourselves, it is the gift of God—not by works, so that no one can boast."

—Ephesians 2:8-9 NIV

Illustration B

This illustration shows us clearly the reality of what Scripture teaches: Jesus is the only way to the Father. In John 14:6 (NIV) Jesus Himself confirms this stating, "I am the way and the truth and the life. No one comes to the Father except through me."

Now if you have believed differently, you may not like Jesus' statement. But the fact of the matter is God created heaven and it belongs to Him. Doesn't He have the right to determine how we get there? He loves you intensely and not only wants to spend eternity with you but also have a thriving relationship with you in the here and now. Jesus said,

"For God so loved the world that he gave his one and only Son, that whoever believes in him shall not perish but have eternal life."

—John 3:16 NIV

What are you supposed to believe? That "Christ died for sins once for all, the righteous for the unrighteous, to bring you to God..." (1 Peter 3:18 NIV). Jesus was tempted in every way possible, yet He did not sin (see Hebrews 4:15). He lived a sinless life, died on the cross, and took the punishment for our sins. In fact, he carried our sins and put sin to death in His own body (see 1 Peter 2:24).

By believing Jesus did this for you, your sins are taken away and your relationship with God is restored. He has reached for us through the cross of Christ, making the way for us to come into His loving presence once again. To Him be praise!

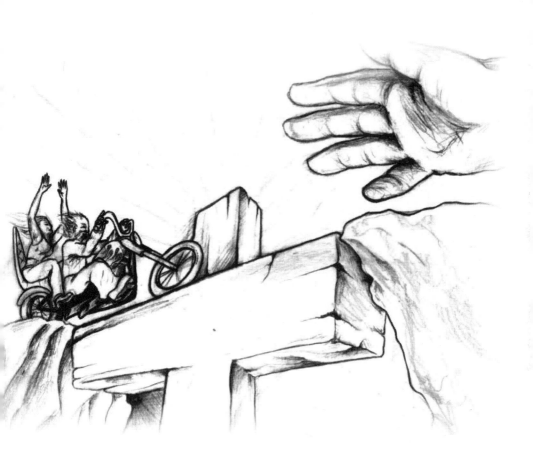

Biker's Prayer

Dear God,

As I begin this ride today, watch over me along the way. Help me to do my very best, to complete this ride, with all the rest. Yet in this race of life, I know, I've made mistakes and stumbled so. But because of Christ's love for me, his death on the cross has set me free. So, as I continue along the way, help me to live the Christ-like way. Though I'm not perfect by any means, with Jesus Christ, I'm on the winning team.

~Author unknown

Prayer to Invite Jesus into Your Heart

"Father God, I come to You just as I am. I've done many things wrong, and I'm a sinner. I ask You to forgive me of everything wrong I've ever done, and wash me clean. Jesus, I believe You are God's Son. Thank You for coming and dying in my place, for my sins. Come and live in my heart. Show me how to live. I need You to lead my life, and I want You to be my best friend. Thank You, Father, for hearing my prayer and forgiving me of my sins. In the name of Your Son, Jesus, Amen."

Recommended Resources

AWESOME BOOKS:

Liberated through Submission: God's Design for Freedom in all Relationships ~ by P.B. Wilson
www.frankandbunny.com/pbwilson.htm

Peace ~ by Joyce Meyer
www.joycemeyer.org

Real Life Answers: Finding Direction for Everyday Challenges ~ by Vincent M. Newfield
www.newfieldscreativeservices.com

The Five Love Languages ~ by Gary Chapman
www.5lovelanguages.com

BIBLE STUDY AND CURRICULUM:
Experiencing God ~ by Henry Blackaby and Claude King
www.blackaby.net

Love & Respect: The Love She Desires and the Respect He Desperately Needs
Book and DVDs ~ by Dr. Emerson Eggerichs,
www.loveandrespect.com

The Bait of Satan Book & Devotional Workbook ~ by John Bevere
www.messengerinternational.org

WEBSITES:
Focus on the Family
www.focusonthefamily.com

Dr. David Hawkins, *The Relationship Doctor*
www.yourrelationshipdoctor.com

Joyce Meyer Ministries
www.joycemeyer.org

One of the greatest resources I recommend is a Bible-believing, Christ-centered local church. We encourage you to find one that you can call home and attend regularly.

To: O Mary

My friend,

Girl the respect I have for you is Huge! :)

Ginormous (sp?)

Blessings d. Joy to you as you press into all the "Sweet Spots" God has created just for you!

Love Ya Lady.

Rena Hanson

Isaiah 41:13